The Female Woman

The Female Woman

ARIANNA STASSINOPOULOS

Random House   New York

Grateful acknowledgment is made to the following for permission to reprint material previously published:

McGraw-Hill Book Company for excerpts from The Female Eunuch, by Germaine Greer. Copyright © 1970, 1971 by Germaine Greer. Published in the United States by McGraw-Hill Book Company.
Doubleday & Company, Inc., for excerpts from Sexual Politics, by Kate Millett. Copyright © 1969, 1970 by Kate Millett.

First American Edition

Library of Congress Cataloging in Publication Data
Stassinopoulos, Arianna, 1950–
   The female woman.
   Bibliography: p.
   1. Women's Liberation Movement. 2. Woman—Social and moral questions. I. Title.
HQ1154.S65   1974   301.41'2   73-20579
ISBN 0-394-49121-1

Manufactured in the United States of America

98765432

To Elli, my mother

Acknowledgments

Until I came to write this book, I didn't really understand why authors publicize their thanks to their friends. I know now how dependent I was on their help and their suggestions. I would particularly like to thank David Powell, who has regularly been sending me "liberated" information from across the Atlantic; Joseph McCulloch, who has let me read the typescript of his work on the man-woman relationship; Frank Johnson and Tricia Hodgson, who read the final draft of the book and made many useful suggestions; Agapi, my sister, who helped with the footnotes in the middle of the night when even her "primitive" typing was invaluable; Christie Davies and John Selwyn Gummer, who read and commented on the manuscript at various stages. I especially thank Christie for helping me with the taped interviews I used as part of my research for the book, and for lending me the manuscript of his new book, *Permissive Britain: Social Change in the Sixties and Seventies.*

Contents

The Female Woman

The Emancipated Woman

Whether we regard the Women's Liberation movement as a serious threat, a passing convulsion or a fashionable idiocy, it is a
movement that mounts an attack on practically everything that
women value today, and introduces the language and sentiments
of political confrontation into the area of personal relationships;
whether or not it is dangerous, it is certainly offensive and it
needs exploding. My total rejection of Women's Lib may surprise
those familiar with Greek society. The road from tradition-bound
Athens to "infidel"[1] Cambridge would seem to lead naturally
toward the Women's Liberation movement. I grew up in a society
which Women's Lib must regard as a patriarchal purgatory—a
baby-crazy land, a land where the position of the unmarried
woman is precarious, a land where dowries still predominate and
where every husband's chief ambition is to be able to display his
economic prowess by removing his wife from her job.

Having seen a rigid traditional and discriminatory society in
action and then plunged into the self-consciously progressive
world of an English university, I was the obvious, enthusiastic
recipient for the Women's Lib message. An outraged rejection of
the society I came from, and a wholehearted espousal of the

Women's Lib ideology, would provide a very tempting, fashionable and self-righteous justification for my departure from its norms. Instead, I found Women's Lib repulsive: I felt that Women's Lib was not simply a movement for the fuller emancipation of women, it was not concerned only with expanding the freedom and opportunities which English and American women already have, relative to their Greek counterparts. It is not a movement calling for equal opportunities, equal pay, equal status for woman's role in life, in fact as well as in law; instead it attacks the very nature of women, and in the guise of liberation, seeks to enslave her.

I have no doubt that there is a great need to combat the prejudice and social conventions that still impose on women a purely traditional role which conflicts with the changed economic and social conditions. But this is the domain and plea of emancipation. Liberation makes claims and demands that go far beyond this;[2] it completely rejects the "otherness" of men and women and seeks to abolish all differences between them. All such differences are *defined* as harmful, as inflicted on women by men, and as the result of social conditioning, never of inherent factors and qualities. It is a short step from such beliefs to advocacy of sexual politics, of bitter conflict between men and women. Men are defined as the enemy, not as human beings to be persuaded, but as an adversary to be fought. I found and find this introduction of the language of politics and conflict into the realm of personal relationships between the sexes utterly objectionable. Equally objectionable is the contempt the "liberated" élite shows for the great mass of "unliberated" women, and for all distinctively female qualities, attitudes and values. Their contempt for these specifically female qualities stems from their belief that these qualities are totally incompatible with the intelligence and self-reliance which, for them, are the paramount virtues.

The truth is that there is no contradiction between femaleness[3] and independence; between femaleness and self-realization; between femaleness and intelligence—today's female woman inte-

4

grates and fuses these qualities without strain, without inner conflict. The "female woman" is not an abstract concept derived from a grand theory. There is no stark dichotomy here, as there is between the liberated superwoman of the Women's Lib Utopia and the women we see every day—the ideal of the female woman is an extension of what we are and does not involve the favorite sport of Women's Lib, the denigration of women as they are today:

The adult woman has already established a pattern of perversity in the expression of her desires and motives which ought to fit her for the distorted version of motherhood: it will not disappear if she is allowed alternatives. Any substituted aim is likely to be followed in a "feminine" way, that is, servilely, dishonestly, inefficiently, inconsistently.[4]

. . . a lifetime of camouflage and idiotic ritual, full of forebodings and failure . . .[5]

. . . all human (as distinct from biological or reproductive) pursuits interesting or uninteresting, [are] designated male "territory". . .[6]

Sexual politics obtains consent through the "socialization" of both sexes to basic patriarchal politics with regard to temperament, role and status . . . The first item temperament involves is the formation of human personality along stereotyped lines of sex category ("masculine" and "feminine") based on the needs and values of the dominant group and dictated by what its members cherish in themselves and find convenient in subordinates: aggression, intelligence, force and efficacy in the male; passivity, ignorance, docility, virtue and ineffectuality in the female.[7]

None of these is meant as a description of a small, odd, atypical group but all are applied in their entirety to most women. If you are an average female reader of this book, you are seen by the leaders of Women's Lib as perverse, servile, dishonest, inefficient, inconsistent, idiotic, passive, ignorant and ineffectual. The moral excuse for this display of contempt and derision is that

5

women are not responsible for their condition; Women's Libbers can safely revile all other women by portraying them as the victims of a male-dominated society. Whatever the excuse, these remarks reveal a deep contempt for women, and for all concepts of womanhood which differ in the least from the Women's Lib ideal. Indeed, they despise the present world of women so much that their Utopia could not possibly incorporate any part of it. After all, who would wish to preserve what is valued by a group so perverse, servile, dishonest and ignorant?

Of the insulting characteristics ascribed to the female by the Libbers—passivity, ignorance, docility, virtue, ineffectuality—one, virtue, seems out of place. Yet it is very clear that Women's Lib regards virtue, altruism and sacrifice as signs of weakness, as the marks of a slave mentality. It weighs up the world in terms of sheer utilitarian egotism. "Ultimately the greatest service a woman can do her community is to be happy"[8]—much like Adam Smith's butcher. The "pursuit of happiness" rides again, but now it is harnessed to the needs of a more passive, sedentary group. Even marriage is seen not as a deep human relationship, but as two separate individuals consuming two separate meals of "satisfaction"—as utility for two. Altruism is neatly disposed of by a piece of crude reductionism:[9] all unselfish acts are really selfish, since they are performed to appease one's conscience, to enter into a commercial arrangement of favors and counterfavors, to please a person who is so close as to be an extension of oneself. Altruism in their view is inauthentic, but what is worse, it is less satisfying than selfishness. The ideal which is to replace altruism is the autonomous, calculated search for individual self-realization—relationships are seen simply as an aspect of the individual's egocentric fixation. This crude view of ethics underlies their concept of society as a whole as well as of specific personal ties; it leads them to see the relationship between the sexes purely in terms of confrontation. The hard egoism of one group is pitted against the newly awakened self-interest of the other. Beyond the struggle lies a diffuse harmony, characterized by a vague love for mankind, and uninterrupted by more intense feelings for particular individuals. The harmony is rarely depicted, but the struggle is painted in all too vivid colors.

The Female Woman parts company with Women's Liberation because of the fundamental qualitative difference between liberation and emancipation. Liberation is not an extension of emancipation: it is not merely a furthering of women's legal, social and political rights in society. Emancipation insists on equal status for distinctively female roles. Liberation demands the abolition of any such distinctive roles: the achievement of equality through identical patterns of behavior.[10] Emancipation means the removal of all barriers to female opportunities—it does not mean compelling women into male roles by devaluing female ones. It means adults freely choosing the way they run their own lives— it does not mean children being brought up without any clear models to follow. It refuses to allow the state to set out deliberately to alter the early upbringing of children so as to enforce greater sameness between the sexes. The fanatical dolls-for-boys-and-engines-for-girls brigade should be firmly resisted, and children allowed to grow up as boys or as girls, without being confused and cross-pressured by interfering liberators. Of course there will always be individuals unable or unwilling to fit into the commonly accepted male and female patterns of behavior. Society must firmly recognize and accept their right to diverge from the norm.

It is curious that the Libbers, who in all other contexts are solely concerned with the individual, exalt the group when it comes to dealing with opportunity and performance. Emancipation demands that all individuals must have access to equal opportunities. The liberators want all groups to perform equally well. The believers in emancipation recognize that there are innate differences between men and women, but stress that an individual's opportunities cannot be formally determined in advance by group characteristics—this is our test of whether discrimination is present or not. The believers in liberation deny that any innate differences exist and declare that unless there are equal numbers of men and women in all jobs and at all levels, discrimination must exist. If women are to be equally represented in all occupations, they must be compelled to adopt all male values and repudiate whatever they have in them that is "different."

With the arrogance of their detached intellectualism, the Women's Libbers fail to draw a distinction between an exciting career and an average, run-of-the-mill, nine-to-five job. They become so intoxicated with their own vehemence against the roles of woman as wife and mother that they endow *any* job outside the family with the qualities of nonstop fascination that very few jobs do, in fact, possess. In idealizing institutionalized work, they seem to yearn after a kind of security that comes from the familiar routine of conventional masculine work. This is not only wrong in itself, it is also a peculiarly anachronistic sentiment at a time when there is a move away from manufacturing toward service industries. In such a service society, expressive roles acquire a much greater importance. In any small group, whether the family, an expedition or the work unit, both instrumental and expressive leaders are needed—one pushing to get things done, the other holding the group together. Traditional manufacturing industry has had far more use for instrumental qualities and instrumental leaders, but in a society geared to the sale or provision of services, the emphasis will shift. The nature of the work, the size of the work group, the needs of the customer, client or recipient, all change and expressive qualities become far more important: it is these qualities that Women's Lib derides as distinctively female and that emancipation recognizes and encourages.

Liberation is a doctrine of mass egotism—emancipation stresses individual fulfillment, but it recognizes that this is best achieved within a framework of relationships and secure mutual expectations. Liberation is only concerned with the individual's frustration at not fulfilling his full potential—it ignores the fact

8

that in prosperous societies, the most important growing problem is not frustration, but meaninglessness. Increasingly the unfulfilled individual is not someone prevented from doing what he wants, but someone who suspects that nothing he wants or can do is really worthwhile. Historically emancipation, by presenting women with a wider choice of life styles, has weakened the security of having one definite pattern to follow. One index of the new uncertainty, and the loosening of group ties that inevitably accompanied these new freedoms, has been the steady rise in the female suicide rate since the end of the nineteenth century.[11] The male rate has, overall, remained steady at a higher level, reflecting the man's even greater but relatively unchanging degree of uncertainty and potential social isolation. The result has been a steady narrowing of the gap between the two rates. Perhaps when the two meet we can say that women are as "emancipated" as men and that the degree of choice, freedom and variety they enjoy is essentially similar. This does not mean that their roles will be identical, merely that they will have to make equally demanding and complex choices between competing roles. Men will remain men, and women will remain women, but their maleness and femaleness will be expressed in a bewildering variety of ways.

Liberation involves a qualitatively different challenge to the individual's sexual identity which would precipitate a chronic state of anomie for both men and women. This acute sense of insecurity, as specific expectations of behavior from men and women become blurred, would create a pattern of diffuse anxiety, of a general sense of meaninglessness. To the question "Who am I?" an individual would no longer even be able to reply: a man, or a woman.

A favorite tactic in argument of experienced Women's Lib casuists is to compare woman's position in society with that of "other deprived groups"—the poor, the blacks, slaves, untouchables.[12] Although women considerably outnumber men in all industrial societies, Women's Lib, in a new arithmetic all their

9

own, regard women as a deprived minority group. The success of the movement seems assured—women wield the strength of being in the majority and yet gain all the rhetorical power which accrues to the underdog by being thought of as a minority. The strategy for success advocated by many of the more radical Women's Libbers is to team up with other minorities in a grand coalition of the underprivileged. It is difficult, though, to see why these real "underclasses" should feel a sense of solidarity with women as a group, for their social situation is totally different. The comparison merely gives the Women's Lib movement an added spurious radicalism, an easy access to the rhetoric of inequality and deprivation.

If women remain an underclass in industrial societies, they must be the only such group that lives longer, owns more wealth and enjoys more deference than its oppressors. In general, in modern societies the upper classes live longer than the middle classes, who in turn live longer than the working classes, and all successfully outlive the poor and destitute. This is especially true of America, where the whites considerably outlive the blacks. Ironically, the converse is true of men and women, for the poor downtrodden woman can expect to outlive her male oppressor by several years.[13] Recently one of the pioneers of women's education who was prevented by the regulations of the time from taking her degree at the end of her examinations at Oxford was given an honorary M.A. by the university at the age of one hundred—all the men who graduated when she should have done have long been dead.[14]

Another index of how inappropriate the rhetoric of inequality is when applied to women is that they own collectively over half the wealth of the richest country in the world. In part their ownership is nominal, the titles of the wealth being in their names for tax purposes. But few oppressors would place their wealth in the hands of the oppressed in this dangerous fashion. Middle-class widows in America may not be merry but they are one of the wealthiest groups in the country, and the average woman can

expect to be a widow for eight years. What is a striking refutation
of the view that it is woman's emotional life that is dependent on
man is the death rate of widowers: 40 percent above the expected
rate for married men, within six months of bereavement![15]

Women's Lib finds the high regard men profess for women
nauseating, and declares that "the chivalrous stance is a game the
master group plays in elevating its subject to pedestal level."[16]
Other real forms of stratification never exhibit this curious permanent inversion of roles.[17] The slave owner, the Brahmin and
the factory owner do not put the slave, the untouchable or the
laborer on a pedestal. Status and virtue are attributes always
reserved for the dominant group, yet men ascribe them to
women. Once again, the Women's Lib rhetoric of inequality is
seen to be bogus, and its moral indignation based on false analo-
gies.

It is true that men hold most of the top political and commercial positions, but it is equally true that in industrial societies,
women often predominate in the three key sources of influence
and power—numbers, wealth and status. Power is not exercised
only through decision making; it can be exercised equally effectively through constraining the decision-making process. It is
simplistic to argue that power is just a matter of the overt decision-making structure, and to confuse the subjective sense of
exercising power enjoyed by the officeholder with the actual
effects of the decisions made and the question of who the benefi-
ciaries of these decisions are.

I have tried to disentangle certain general themes in the
Women's Lib ideology, but it has proved very difficult to establish
the application of these general themes in specific areas. Neither
Women's Liberation as a movement nor any one of its leading
protagonists has put forward a coherent ideological program—
the nature of the movement renders it impossible for them to do
so. There is a millenarian quality about the movement which is
antithetical to rational argument. It is characterized by a belief
that there is an inexorable move toward the stage of liberation

in which all existing structured relationships deeply involving women will disappear. It is paradoxical that this vanguard, with time so assuredly on its side, should exhibit such a hysterical sense of urgency. Because the Women's Lib argument is so chaotic, it is not really possible to attempt to refute it step by step in a syllogistic manner—it can only be dealt with by dealing in turn with the critical common assumptions and propositions that it makes in certain crucial areas. Each section of the book deals with the core arguments of the Women's Liberation movement in the most vital areas.

	WOMEN'S LIB	THE FEMALE WOMAN
Nature	Apart from reproduction, there are no inherent differences between the sexes. Equality is sameness.	There are important innate differences between the sexes. Men and women are equal but different.
Sex	The sexual nature of men and women is identical. Promiscuity is to be encouraged.	There are important differences in the sexual nature of the two sexes. Sex is much more fulfilling within a deep personal relationship.
Femininity	Intelligence and femininity are incompatible.	Intelligence enhances femininity.
The Family	A crumbling institution to be abolished.	An important institution to be fostered.
Work	The whole of life. Only the routine, the efficient, the paid for, is valuable. The mere housewife is contemptible.	A part of life. Women have two equally important fields open to them; their families and their careers—they should be able to choose either or both.

Men	The oppressors, a highly privileged group.	Men's fate is more extreme than women's —sometimes more privileged, sometimes much more deprived.
Liberators	An enlightened élite.	Muddled intellectuals projecting their hang-ups onto all women.

Each of these propositions must be exploded separately, for there is no central structure to the building of Women's Liberation—it is a building without support, where the rooftop of liberation floats mysteriously over entrenched, dogmatic foundations. The roof will, in time, fall of its own accord—it is the more modest purpose of this book to dynamite the foundations.

The Natural Woman

The fundamental tenet of the Women's Lib ideology is that there are no innate differences between men and women—other than reproduction.

> . . . the best medical research points to the conclusion that sexual stereotypes have no bases in biology.[1]

> . . . it is the threadbare tactic of justifying social and temperamental differences by biological ones. For the sexes are inherently in everything alike save reproductive systems, secondary sexual characteristics, orgasmic capacity, and genetic and morphological structure. Perhaps the only things they can uniquely exchange are semen and transudate.[2]

> In order to approximate those shapes and attitudes which are considered normal and desirable, both sexes deform themselves, justifying the process by referring to the primary, genetic difference between the sexes.[3]

These are fine, strident, confident assertions—the confidence displayed is, as with many other ideological polemicists, in inverse proportion to the factual evidence cited or even existing, just like the preacher who wrote against a passage in his notes:

14

"Argument weak—SHOUT." For Women's Libbers there are no facts, there are only ideologically convenient assumptions. The truth is not determined empirically but is defined as that which accords with the aims of their movement and its current ideology. When Kate Millett, author of *Sexual Politics,* descends to dealing with the facts, she undermines her own assertions—indeed, she is *forced* to do so, forced to enumerate a string of exceptions which completely destroy her case. She does not seem aware of how all-pervasive these differences in "genetic and morphological structure" are. Men and women differ in every cell of their bodies,[4] and body and mind are not separate entities in the simple and rigid way the Women's Libbers believe. There is a definitely dated air about the way in which they assume that bodily differences between men and women have no implications for differences in mind and personality.

Those Women's Libbers who are not atheists on the subject of innate differences are militant agnostics. John Stuart Mill is a clear case of the dogmatic agnostic on this: "I deny that anyone knows, or can know the nature of the two sexes."[5] From this position of splendid ignorance he and his followers draw strong policy conclusions. Militant agnosticism is an uncomfortable position from which to pontificate on policy; Mill retreats into an assertion of starkly contradictory nature: "It may be asserted without scruple that no other class of dependants have had their character so entirely distorted from its natural proportions by their relation with their masters."[6]

It is strange that without knowing, or being able to know, what woman's essential nature is, Mill can assert that women differ from it, and by implication in a particular direction. In fact, there is no reason why an agnostic should not believe that society's roles for women do coincide with their essential nature or that their "natural" character is a grotesque exaggeration of society's "stereotypes."

The modern Women's Libbers tend to slip out of agnosticism by a different route: they invert Pascal and argue that in the absence of definite proof that innate sex differences do exist, we should assume that they do not. They seem to believe that to assume zero innate differences between men and women is somehow less arbitrary than accepting any positive statement about their existence based on anything less than a final proof derived from unassailable evidence. Their argument involves a false dichotomy between the view that no innate differences exist and the view that these innate differences correspond exactly to those observed in society. The position of the "nonliberated" believers in emancipation is that differences do exist, that there is no one-to-one correspondence between these and the social roles men and women play, and that opportunities should be adjusted so that there is a greater correspondence between the two.

The Women's Lib explanation for all observed differences between the sexes is standardized, predictable and unvaried—it is all a matter of conditioning. Conditioning is of course "a bad thing" except when it is used to eradicate differences between the sexes. Some of the ways in which men and women behave differently are undoubtedly the result of differential conditioning, and this can be easily observed. The fact that little girls are given dolls to play with and little boys guns has obvious effects on the way they grow up. Naturally, when parents find tears acceptable in daughters and frown upon them in sons, a particular behavior pattern is encouraged. But Women's Lib wishes to extend this form of explanation into areas where no such differential conditioning can be perceived. In the absence of evidence they assert that such conditioning *must* be present in a form too subtle to be detected. As each suggestion on the nature of this conditioning has to be discarded, they retreat into an "infinite regression" of explanation—each explanation assumes a form of conditioning more subtle, more vacuous, more vague, more intangible than the one before. When confronted with the universality of certain sex differences found in diverse societies, diverse cultures and even diverse mammalian species, they postulate an ever more tenuous, ever more pervasive form of conditioning—a modern version of the Victorian "ether," an extreme attempt to remodel the universe to fit the theory.

The universality of conditioning as an explanation is conveniently dropped when a sex difference is discovered that can be explained in terms of the innate superiority of women: "About thirty other disorders [as well as color-blindness] are to be found in the males of the species and seldom in the females for the same reason. There is much evidence that the female is constitutionally stronger than the male . . . There is no explanation for the more frequent conception of males . . . It is tempting to speculate whether this might not be a natural compensation for the greater vulnerability of males."[7]

This quotation from Germaine Greer reveals two characteristic aspects of Women's Lib—inconsistency and malice. Greater vulnerability is graciously conceded, without any difficulty, to be an innate male trait, but any suggestion that this is true of positive qualities like persistence would be hysterically repudiated. There is just such a touch of hysteria about Millett's "the *best* medical research" or "the *most reasonable* . . . sources."[8] She has introduced the superlatives of the advertising industry into scientific research. In fact, she uses the superlative in a way no adman would be allowed by the regulatory agencies. "This week's best buy in endocrinology is. . . ." In Millett's newspeak, "best" is of course defined as "doubleplusgoodwomenslib."[9] Ironically, "best" medical research for Women's Libbers occurred mainly in the period 1930–1960, which Millett has anathematized as the years of the counterrevolution against women. Until 1966 there was "a conspiracy of silence surrounding the topic of human sex differences. During the fifties and early sixties—a period during which some of the most exciting and significant neuroendocrinological studies on mammals were carried out—the literature on human sex differences was extraordinarily sparse. What little there was dealt mainly with the sociological and cultural aspects of sex differences."[10] This was clearly an ideal period for Women's Lib; little research was being done, so disturbing findings were unlikely to be unearthed, and what little research was done was dominated by "nice" American liberals who clung desperately to the prejudice of progressive bigots that "boys are boys and girls are girls because they are reared that way, not because they are born that way."[11]

Researchers in these fields recognized, reluctantly at first and more willingly later, that there are major innate differences between the sexes. Because of the strong ethical reasons against performing experiments on human beings, much of our knowledge of the origins of innate sex differences comes from a study of intersexed persons who, for various accidental reasons, have some of the characteristics of both sexes. Normally, sexual characteristics are determined by the presence or absence of a Y chromosome. If the Y chromosome is present, the fetus normally produces androgen hormones, which determine the development of male characteristics. It is the presence or absence of these androgens at a crucial point in the development of the fetus that determines its sex. What is very important for the demonstration of innate sexual differences is the case where a fetus that is genetically female is accidentally exposed to androgens at this point and develops male characteristics; this happens either as a result of an inborn error of metabolism, or as a side effect of drugs given to the mother during pregnancy. Depending on the amount and timing of exposure to androgens, the fetus is greatly or slightly masculinized. If the degree of masculinization is extreme, the baby will look like a boy and may even be brought up as one.

The significant case, though, is where there is only a slight degree of masculinization and the parents give the child a perfectly ordinary female upbringing which, if Women's Libbers are to be believed, should completely smother any innate masculine tendencies caused by the hormones. Unfortunately for them, a comparison of these girls with a group of normal girls showed that they are far more likely to display masculine behavior and attitudes.[12] From an early age they showed much less interest in playing with dolls and in rehearsing the roles of mother and wife. They were more interested in athletics and outdoor games than the control group. They were rough and competitive with boys and much more likely to get involved in fights. They preferred boys' clothes and toys *despite* strong and consistent pressure from their parents for more feminine behavior. Only one of the control group of normal girls would rather have been a boy, but a large minority of the "masculinized girls" would prefer to have been boys and they all felt very ambivalent about their sex. Even in areas which are assumed to be completely culturally determined, such as the relative evaluation of marriage and a career, they displayed preferences markedly different from the "normal" girls. Their early lack of interest in child care also persisted into adult life.

Experiments with animals confirm what observation of human accidents suggests; by manipulating the level of androgens to which a fetus is exposed before birth, the experimenter can produce male or female behavior in the young animal at will.[13] Not even the most frantic efforts of the mother guinea pig or monkey could reverse this process.

It is well known that men with an extra Y chromosome (XYY) are hypermasculine—very tall, aggressive, impulsive and often violent and delinquent from a very early age.[14] Perhaps, in deference to the feelings of Women's Lib, the popularizers of this genetic relationship have been loath to draw the obvious conclusion that qualities like masculinity are genetically determined, and though they may be culturally reinforced, they are not culturally created. In the same way, an extra X chromosome in a man (XXY) undermines the masculine traits, leads to a subnormal libido and a greater incidence of homosexuality, transvestism and transexualism.[15] The differences in attitudes, behavior and interests between androgenized, masculinized females and normal women can be seen in the opposite direction in the case of a genetic abnormality, Turner's Syndrome, that leads to extreme and exaggerated femininity: "Whereas none of the Turner cases

regarded themselves or were considered by others to be a tomboy, most of the hermaphroditic (i.e., masculinized) cases did so,
and were also regarded so by others. . . . Of the girls with Turner's Syndrome, some put marriage before a career, more
wanted both, but only one put a career before marriage and she
wished to be a nun!"[16] All these characteristics appear long
before the child knows of her condition and often long before it
is diagnosed.

There is simply no way in which this evidence can be as-
similated into the Women's Lib assumption that all differences in
attitudes and behavior are the result of the imposition of artificial
sexual stereotypes by society. Women's Libbers are very fond of
using cases of intersexed patients as evidence that sex roles are
acquired purely by education and upbringing. They point to the
cases of patients of ambiguous sexuality brought up as boys, later
found to be genetically female, turned into anatomical females by
surgery and yet often retaining their male outlook. Here is a
classic case of the Women's Libbers' misinterpretation and
misuse of social and biological evidence to support their fundamental assumptions that all differences between men and women
are culturally determined, and that human beings are infinitely
malleable into masculinity, femininity or some grotesque mixture
of both. What they fail to realize is that in the case of these
intersexed people, the two innate physical factors which determine sex and which normally reinforce one another—chromosomes and hormones—are in conflict and push the individual in
opposite directions. It is inevitable, when this happens, that the
individual is more pliable, more open to purely social forces; it
is not that the social forces are inherently so strong as to be the
determining factor, but that when the physical forces are in conflict, their net effect is greatly weakened, and so the social factors
are able to predominate. They do so because they are reinforced
by one of the two key sets of physical forces; if, for example, a
genetic female is so masculinized by hormones as to look like a
baby boy at birth, it is absurd to assume that only "its" external

appearance has been affected and that social forces are acting on a completely neutral or "really" female being. The truth is that where the external appearance differs from the sex of the chromosomes, everything else differs also—the brain, the central nervous system, the very being of the child have been affected in the same direction as the child's external appearance. The individual accepts an upbringing contrary to "its" chromosomes because in many ways it is already innately fitted for it.

One of the most striking differences between men and women —the much greater individual variability of men—provides additional strong evidence for the existence of innate differences between the sexes. Men are less average than women.[17] They are the geniuses and the idiots, the giants and the dwarfs; although women are, on an average, shorter than men, it is always Snow White who towers over the seven dwarfs, almost always male dwarfs who feature in circuses and pantomimes. The greater variability of men cannot possibly be explained on environmental grounds, as a simple difference in averages might be. If women are not found in the top positions in society in the same proportions as men because, as Women's Lib claims, they are treated as mentally inferior to men and become so, why are there so many more male idiots? Why are the remedial classes in schools full of boys? Why are the inmates of hospitals for the mentally subnormal predominantly male? Discrimination produces a consistency of inferiority, not a greater concentration around a common average—fewer at the top but *also* fewer at the bottom.

The reason why Women's Lib does not mention this conspicuous difference between the sexes is that it can only be explained on purely biological grounds. The male Y chromosome induces greater genetic variety,[18] and at all stages of growth the development of the male is slower with more time for variation to occur: "The delay in the emergence of a characteristic suggests that the variance of that characteristic for males will be greater than that for females. Relatively more males will be represented at the extreme of the spread of the characteristic."[19]

Women's Lib, of course, refuses to acknowledge any of these differences; the only difference they effectively admit is the one between male and female reproductive systems, a difference which they might have some slight difficulty in denying. However, reproduction is safely relegated to a totally unimportant position in their new scale of values. The idea that there may be other differences, particularly in the sacred area of the brain and the central nervous system, is anathema; they have a chronic fear that if any such differences were proven, women would necessarily be shown to be inferior. Such is their faith in woman's nature that it never occurs to them that the differences might be in her favor. The very idea of highly differentiated reproductive systems in the same body as identical brain and nervous systems is endocrinological nonsense: ". . . the sex hormones seem to exert a double action on the central nervous system. First, during foetal or neonatal life, these hormones seem to act in an inductive way on an undifferentiated brain (as they do on the undifferentiated genital tract) to organize it to a 'male type' or 'female type' of brain. And second, during adult existence the gonadal (sex) hormones act on the central nervous system in an excitatory or inhibitory way. . . ."[20]

This must be a severe shock to Women's Libbers. They have a remarkably Victorian attitude to the reproductive system: it must be kept rigidly apart from the purer, higher organs of mind and sensibility. Once again, the reproductive system is nasty, evil and utterly unimportant—not this time because sex is wicked, but because the reproductive system is a horrid reminder of the fundamental differences between men and women. The extremists among the Victorians wished they could have reproduction without sex; the extremists among Women's Lib would like reproduction without women—test tubes have the virtue of not reminding women of their distinctiveness.[21]

With characteristic misplaced certainty, Germaine Greer writes of "the failure of fifty years of thorough and diversified testing to discover any pattern of differentiation in male and female intellectual powers."[22] While Miss Greer was pontificating, psychologists were busy trying to establish the reasons for the marked differences in the various types of ability between boys and girls, men and women. Why should girls display greater ability in tests of verbal intelligence, and boys greater ability in nonverbal tests? The early inferiority of boys in verbal skills is displayed in an exaggerated form in cases of childhood abnormalities. Boys are more likely to be autistic and to become withdrawn because they are unable to comprehend and act on the verbal messages that the world presses on them. Boys learn to talk later, learn to read later and often with great difficulty. The gap between verbal and nonverbal ability common among boys is even greater among juvenile delinquents.[23] This delinquent gap reflects the exaggerated masculinity of these children manifest in their highly "male" pattern of abilities, their aggressiveness and their uncooperative nature. Their lack of verbal abilities makes it difficult for these boys to cope with social situations, with relationships, with learning, with school; at the same time their other abilities enable them to be a successful disruptive influence, and the larger the gap, the greater the likelihood of delinquency.

The superior verbal ability of girls and their steadier linguistic development has the result that "intellectual development in girls takes place primarily through linguistic channels and that the development is a fairly consistent one; in boys, however, the non-verbal skills clearly play a prominent but less predictable part in their intellectual development."[24] In other words, boys and girls learn differently, and this difference cannot be dismissed as simply yet another aspect of the male plot to keep women intellectually subservient. Generally it is in culturally favored groups that verbal abilities are greater than nonverbal ones. Women's Lib is faced with the uncomfortable alternative of either admitting that education, culture and society discriminate in favor of women or conceding that this key difference in intellectual abilities is innate.

Women's Libbers are, of course, notoriously asymmetrical in the phenomena they observe and protest about. Female superiority in verbal skills is not likely to be a subject of their wrath. If men's achievements are inferior—too bad! The male superiority in nonverbal skills is much more likely to be a target for these female chauvinists. One important type of nonverbal ability is spatial ability—seen in a boy or a chimpanzee throwing at a target, a rat exploring a maze, a child completing a pattern in an intelligence test, or a man assembling a design, all activities which "demand the perception and use of spatial relationships,"[25] and the ability to pick them out against a misleading background. In all these skills, males are likely to be superior— indeed, greater spatial ability has been found in male babies as young as two weeks old.[26] These are abilities genetically determined, "which cultural factors seem to affect hardly at all";[27] "the fact of the development of sex differences in spatial ability by the sex chromosomes would appear to be beyond doubt."[28] In West Africa, men suffering from a disease induced by protein deficiency in infancy become feminized even to the extent of developing breasts—these men show lower spatial and numerical ability than normal men, but their verbal ability is actually *greater*. They exhibit a female pattern of abilities, not as a result of cultural conditioning but because of an endocrinal disorder—clear evidence for sex differences in ability being determined by innate hormonal differences.[29]

Germaine Greer, who took a hard "atheist's" line on the existence of differences in male and female abilities, becomes cautiously agnostic on the subject of the brain and the way it affects these abilities: "The brain is so imperfectly understood that we simply do not know enough about its physiology and function to deduce facts about performance."[30] There is nothing like wishful ignorance, a stone unturned for fear of the nasty insects that lie beneath it! Recent research does, in fact, show that there is a relationship between sex differences in abilities and the structure of the brain. There is a clear link between the earlier and greater lateralization of brain function in females and their greater verbal and inferior spatial aptitudes. Children write with a preferred hand—they are right-handed or left-handed—not because of any intrinsic difference in their hands but because one side of their brain is dominant and controls that activity; other similar "lateralizations" occur in the brain, and one side of the brain comes to dominate all verbal activities. This process is "accelerated in the female brain" and so "facilitates the development of linguistic skill in women."[31]

Women's Lib would be equally livid with the findings of studies showing a close relationship between hormone levels and various other skills and abilities. Men with high androgen levels—identified by their excretion of certain chemicals, their thickset physique with large chests and biceps, their large amount of pubic hair—show a marked superiority in persistence[32] and in "automatized" behavior.[33] It is easy to see the relationship of persistence with success in a competitive society. Automatization ability is also clearly related to occupational achievement; such ability refers to behaviors "which have been so highly practised that minimums of mental and physical effort are required for their efficient execution. Such behaviours include the bulk of everyday activities, e.g., keeping one's balance, walking, talking, reading. . . . Automatization of simple habits is a *pre-requisite* for the acquisition of new, more complex abilities. . . ."[34]

It is hardly surprising that these qualities are highly valued and important for success in a complex industrial society. Women's Lib becomes hysterical at the fact that these qualities are found predominantly in men. What will they do in the face of evidence that these qualities are largely hormonally determined? Will they dose their daughters with androgens?[35] Will they pray for them to develop large biceps and hairy chests? They completely forget that for every positive male quality or ability there is a positive but neglected female counterpart. The high androgen levels which aid automatization have a negative effect on other abilities, such as restructuring; the opposite of persistence is distractability

—in our industrial society with its cult of single-mindedness and specialization, this concept may have a negative ring about it, but it really refers to a woman's ability, while performing one task, to be alert to the demands of several others.

When the psychologists calculated the average IQ scores, they *chose* to make the average the same for both men and women at 100 by giving appropriate weights to their scores on the different tests—by effectively attaching equal importance to male and female abilities. This is hardly the behavior of the male chauvinist conspiracy that Women's Lib sees in all academic psychology. What the psychologists "refused" to be was a part of a Women's Lib conspiracy to demonstrate equality between the sexes by concealing all differences in ability rather than by acknowledging them and weighting their results accordingly.

Perhaps there is a moral here for society. It would be futile to attempt to fit women into a masculine pattern of attitudes, skills and abilities, and disastrous to force them to suppress their specifically female characteristics and abilities by keeping up the pretense that there are no differences between the sexes. These differences should be recognized and society's activities molded in a way that makes full use of both male and female qualities. It is ironic that as society's economic base shifts away from manufactures and toward services, creating a much greater need for distinctively female personal skills, there should be such a clamor for women to acquire the talents of a manufacturing society. It is equally ironic that at a time when the overspecialization and impersonality of such a society are being questioned and criticized, Women's Lib should idealize the very skills and qualities that both create such a society and are a product of it. Women have a greater complexity and competence in thought, feeling and observation in relation to people, a more protective and less belligerent attitude to the world and a distinctive interest in personal relationships rather than objects; women's superiority in verbal skills is an important aspect of this female emphasis on relationships.[36] All these are qualities uniquely suited to the needs of the emerging service society.

Nowhere is the female emphasis on relationships more important that in the expression of their sexuality. For Germaine Greer, "the 'normal' sex roles that we learn to play from our infancy are no more natural than the antics of a transvestite."[37] These "unnatural" normal sex roles are strongly geared toward personal relationships and the needs and qualities of the female personality. If this is what Germaine Greer derides as normality, then let us all try to be more and more normal! To suggest that the antics of the transvestite are of the same nature as the personal relationships in which normal—not "normal"—sex roles are embodied is too fatuous even to provide the shock effect clearly intended. The transvestite's antics are directed not at a loved person but at the ludicrously outdated suspender belts, spike heels, bouffant wigs, corsets, etc. The general male mastery over objects and the ability to create and manipulate impersonal situations spill over into their sexuality. These innate male characteristics penetrate not only men's occupational roles but the sexual aspects of their lives and personalities. There is a great deal of independent evidence to show that the differences in male and female sexual behavior and attitudes are largely innate and not the result of discriminatory sexual stereotypes.[38]

Equally, there is substantial and varied evidence to show that men are innately more aggressive than women—a fact that drives liberated women to be *almost* as aggressive as men: "In contemporary terminology, the basic division of temperamental trait is marshalled along the line of 'aggression is male' and 'passivity is female.' . . . If aggressiveness is the trait of the master class, docility must be the corresponding trait of a subject group."[39] It is not difficult to see why this atypical minority of hyperaggressive women should have a big stake in the conspiracy theory of the origin and maintenance of temperamental differences between the sexes. Loaded terms like "master" and "subject" are simply an attempt to mystify, conceal and discredit the existence of different levels of aggressiveness in men and women.

In all primates, the male is stronger and more aggressive than the female, and this is especially true where they differ markedly in size and appearance. Among gibbons, the male and female do not differ markedly in appearance: the male is only slightly the more aggressive, and the division of labor is much less rigid in gibbon society than among other apes and monkeys. Among baboons, the male is much the larger, it has a highly distinctive appearance, and it is much the more aggressive. Human beings resemble the baboons rather than the gibbons(!) with their large differences in size and mass and such prominent secondary sexual characteristics as breasts and beards.[40] Indeed, a Martian biologist could be forgiven for believing that men and women belonged to different species, one far more aggressive than the other.

Male aggressiveness can be stimulated by the administration of male hormones, and prenatal exposure to androgens can induce subsequent masculine aggressiveness even in a female. However, "the male hormone facilitates the expression of aggression but only in an individual who has already differentiated as a male."[41] Women's Libbers cannot acquire this vaunted quality by dosing themselves, though those who become pregnant might seek the appropriate pharmacological environment for the fetus so as to ensure that any girl born to them has her full share of male pugnacity. Unfortunately, in the absence of accurate sex tests for babies, they might erroneously produce a hyperaggressive boy— a male chauvinist piglet with the instincts of a wild boar.

Even at an early age, small boys are more aggressive and exploratory than girls and are far less sensitive to pain—they display and elicit much more frequent and more prolonged outbursts of aggression. Even at the age of thirteen months, girls are less adventurous; in a playroom they are more reluctant to leave their mothers, return to her after a shorter interval, approach her for reassurance more often and spend far more time in the area nearest to her. "When a wire mesh barrier was introduced half-way across the room separating infant from mother, boys and girls reacted quite differently: the girls cried much more than the boys and typically stood at the centre of the barrier waiting help-lessly whilst the boys made active attempts even when distressed to get round the ends of the barrier to return to the mother."[42] "Early conditioning into helpless dependence!" scream the Women's Lib harpies. But these sex differences in behavior are found even where no conditioning could possibly occur, as with infant monkeys reared with wire-and-cloth "inanimate surrogate mothers." Even among these liberated monkeys, "male infants after the first three weeks of life threaten other animals much more frequently than do female infants; on the other hand females reared in isolation show a similar tendency to passivity and rigidity. Rough and tumble play increases during the first three months but is always engaged in more by male than female infants; in fact, deprivation of social experience seems to enhance the sex differences."[43] Sex-linked differences in behavior do not persist only among liberated monkeys, they also persist among liberated children in the kibbutz paradise of undifferentiated up-bringing: "In all age groups girls are more integrative (helpful, affectionate, co-operative) than boys, and boys more disintegra-tive. In all groups boys engage in more acts of conflict than girls, and in all but one group the boys engage in more acts of aggres-sion than girls."[44]

All these innate differences reflect the basic historical division of labor between the sexes; the exact nature of the division has varied, but in general men have been the hunters and fighters, women have brought up the children. Today, most activities do not fit into this simple division, and women's fuller emancipation is a necessity not only for their greater fulfillment but for the more effective working of society. Women's Libbers are always ready to point at this breakdown of the traditional division of labor, and proclaim that men and women are becoming increas-ingly alike and ought to be indistinguishable. What they ignore is that the conditions leading to the erosion of the traditional division of labor have existed only since the beginning of agriculture, and the changes only became rapid after the industrial revolution—a very small fragment of human history compared to the millions of years of human existence. Culturally we are now "industrial men and women," but genetically we still carry within us the hunters and the childbearers—our not so distant ancestors. We could not possibly have had sufficient time to evolve genetically away from our ancestral model. Men have been hunters for *several million* years. Settled agriculture has only existed for some thousands of years, and industry about two hundred—mere seconds in evolutionary and geological time.

It is inconceivable that millions of years of evolutionary selection during a period of a marked sexual division of labor have not left pronounced traces on the innate character of men and women. Aggressiveness, and mechanical and spatial skills, a sense of direction, and physical strength—all masculine characteristics—are the qualities essential for a hunter; even food gatherers need these same qualities for defense and exploration. The prolonged period of dependence of human children, the difficulty of carrying the peculiarly heavy and inert human baby—a much heavier, clumsier burden than the monkey infant and much less able to cling on for safety—meant that women could not both look after their children and be hunters and explorers. Early humans learned to take advantage of this period of dependence to transmit rules, knowledge and skills to their offspring—women needed to develop verbal skills, a talent for personal relationships, and a predilection for nurturing going even beyond the maternal instinct. The survival of the core of these qualities in the form of specifically female innate characteristics can easily be seen in women's everyday behavior; evidence that these characteristics are, in fact, innate can be deduced from the behavior of females at an age so young that the "all-pervasive" conditioning could not have had time to intrude: "Even at three days of age babies are more responsive to the cry of another baby than to an artificially produced sound of the same intensity, and girl babies are more responsive in this respect than boy babies."[45] The girls' greater responsiveness to such sounds is confirmed by the fact that it is possible to establish conditioned reflexes in baby girls at the age of fourteen weeks using sounds as the reinforcement, while baby boys of the same age can only be similarly conditioned using visual stimuli. It is as if the girls are responsive to sounds in the same way a mother has to be; the boys react rather to visual stimuli like their hunting ancestors.[46]

For millions of years we have carried within us an innate maleness or femaleness which was created and adapted over a period of time vastly outside the time scale of social engineers, outside the time horizon of even the most Utopian plans. Even if Women's Lib was given a hundred, a thousand, ten thousand years in which to eradicate *all* the differences between the sexes, it would still be an impossible undertaking. Perhaps if they were given millions of years they would reach their Utopia, but then, in the long run, we are all fossils. What Women's Lib might achieve if their "consciousness-raising"—or in plain English, brainwashing—campaign succeeds is a society whose members have identical roles but are perpetually at war with themselves; a society of males made neurotic by suppressed masculinity, of females made miserable by having masculine roles thrust upon them that contradict their feminine impulses.

The basic Women's Lib assumption that underlies all their theorizing, their ideology, their prescriptions for social reform is that men and women are infinitely malleable. This is the assumption that expresses itself in demands for "a systematic reformation of [people's] lives that refuses aprioristic systematization but moves through phases of de-structuring, un-conditioning, de-educating and de-familiarizing ourselves so that we at last get on familiar but unfamilial terms with ourselves and are then ready to re-structure ourselves in a manner that refuses all personal taboos and consequently will revolutionize the whole society."[47] Evolution, observation, experiment all prove that no amount of de-structuring, un-conditioning and de-educating will eradicate the differences between the sexes. All evidence shows that to refer to certain needs and desires as "natural" does not mean apologetically retreating into question-begging clichés. Here there are two opposing views of what man is and what woman is. The Women's Lib view asserts that there are false needs and true needs and that women have been bludgeoned and coerced into denying their true needs and accepting false substitutes; the very nature of their case is suspect because no evidence can be adduced to support the distinction they make between true and false. The alternative view, which sees the world in terms of the "natural," a view summed up in the concept of "the female woman," involves a value judgment in the same way, but it is at least rooted in the real world of fact, evidence and observation. The truth will make you free, but only if you have a way of ascertaining just what the truth is.

The Sexual Woman

A girl (how many girls?) was raped last month by more than eighty Pakistani soldiers and went out of her mind. How many men can truly say they see no connection, however small, between this extreme event and their own occasional behaviour?

—JILL TWEEDIE[1]

Men may well fail to see this connection, but for Women's Libbers it is far from small. Indeed, most of their tracts are filled with lurid descriptions of brutal male sexuality culled from a wide range of authors that includes Norman Mailer and Henry Miller and Henry Miller and Norman Mailer. These authors revel in explicit descriptions of brutal sexual activities. Women are treated as objects, not as persons, and the key aspect of sexuality is sadistic domination by the male. For the hard-line Women's Libbers, the connection is not an occasional one (as it is for Jill Tweedie) but an inevitable and all-pervasive one.

In reality what Miller and Mailer depict is an exaggeration and distortion of the sexual lives that most people lead. Indeed, often their descriptions are not even exaggerations but outright fantasy. It is absurd to infer from these extreme cases of male sexual dominance that all male sexuality is so repulsively brutal. The Women's Lib argument is based on a false antithesis of idealized equality contrasted with total domination by the male and total submission by the female. Or else, a little more subtly, the argument runs on these lines: extreme domination is repellent; a small element of this is present in all male-female sexual relations, therefore they are also repellent.[2] This is nonsense—many things which are unpleasant or downright dangerous in large doses are welcome in small ones: salt, alcohol, heat, excitement. Even arsenic is present in eggs! The relationship between the degree of fulfillment felt by two people as a result of their sexual involvement, and the degree of dominance and submission present, are much more complex. In societies where there is a very high level of male dominance, as in the *machismo* cult of Latin America[3] or certain mining communities,[4] sex is not an enjoyable or fulfilling experience for the woman. But it is also true that where the men are totally lacking in aggressive virility, sex is not an enjoyable experience for either partner.[5] Psychiatrists' clinics are filled with excessively gentle, unaggressive men sent there by their frustrated and dissatisfied wives. The very act of sex itself precludes the idealized form of sexual equality advocated by Women's Lib.

Some degree of male dominance is necessary in sexual relationships, but society is very careful to control and limit it. The very instances of male dominance cited by Kate Millett—rape, heterosexual sodomy, indecent assault, maiming[6]—are forbidden by our supposedly patriarchal society.[7] Pimps and brothel keepers are treated with great harshness by society precisely because they are thought to be exploiters of women in the way Millett decries. Indeed, Millett's indignation is very little different from that of Queen Victoria. When it comes to brutal and perverse sexuality Kate Millett tries to have it both ways! She damns both society and the activities that society condemns.

Germaine Greer, too, wants it both ways. She quotes the book

Last Exit to Brooklyn as creating feelings of "guilt" in its readers, implying that the rape scene she quotes was an integral part of their sexual experience:

> . . . more came forty maybe fifty and they screwed her and went back on line and had a beer and yelled and laughed and someone yelled that the car stunk of cunt so Tralala and the seat were taken out of the car and laid in the lot and she lay there naked on the seat and their shadows hid her pimples and scabs and she drank flipping her tits with the other hand and somebody shoved the beer can against her mouth and they all laughed and Tralala cursed and spit out a piece of tooth and someone shoved it again . . . and the next one mounted her and her lips were split this time . . .[8]

Germaine Greer uses this quotation from Hubert Selby to demonstrate "the survival of cunt hatred in our society."[9] By implication, Tralala is the innocent victim of man's monopoly of brutal violence. Yet only a few pages before, we read that "Tralala stomped on his face until both eyes were bleeding and his nose was split and broken, then knocked him a few times in the balls."[10]

More important, nowhere does Germaine Greer mention the reaction of society to crimes of this nature. A mass rape of this kind by Hell's Angels in England recently led to the men receiving several years in jail. The judge commented: "No man could have listened in this court over the last four days without a feeling of horror and shame that persons in this country could behave like you three. . . . You made a spectacle of your rape, degrading her for gratification and entertainment of the others who were there, and as she said, sort of laughing as it happened. If I had not heard the descriptions of what went on, I would not have believed that human beings could have behaved in this way . . . What happened was about as bad as anything could have been —as vile and horrible as anything."[11]

Here the judge speaks for all except a tiny, twisted minority of people. Rape is abhorrent to most men and they are genuinely filled with "shock and alarm,"[12] and not because they secretly wish to be rapists themselves. It is a moral sentiment that is founded not on guilt, but on humanity. Men are neither beasts who hate women nor cowards who would like to. They are simply people with a similar ability as women to feel compassion and indignation at an outrage.

It is curious that the libertarians in society support Women's Lib and wish to legalize the pornography that extols the very aspects or potential aspects of male sexual behavior that Women's Libbers abhor. It is those who uphold traditional "patriarchal" standards who wish to restrain the male potential for promiscuity, violence and exploitation. Could it be that what many Women's Libbers want is equal access to male fantasy? Promiscuity, violence, exploitation are all right provided both sexes can exercise them. They would create a world in which sex is "solitary, poor, nasty, brutish and short."[13] It does not need a Hobbes to point out the dangers of a sex war of all against all.

The absurdity of Millett's use of Miller and Mailer as representative pictures of everyday sex life fades into insignificance when compared to her use of the homosexual world portrayed by Jean Genet as an analogue of heterosexual relations. She writes: "Because of the perfection with which they ape and exaggerate the 'masculine' and 'feminine' of heterosexual society, his homosexual characters represent the best contemporary insight into its constitution and beliefs. Granted that their caricature is grotesque, and Genet himself is fully aware of the morbidity of this pastiche, his homosexuals nonetheless have unerringly penetrated to the essence of what heterosexual society imagines to be the character of 'masculine' and 'feminine' . . . a description of what it is to be female as reflected in the mirror society of homosexuality. But the passage only implies what it is to be male. It is to be master, hero, brute and pimp, which is also to be irremediably stupid and cowardly. In this feudal relationship of male and female, pimp and queen, one might expect exchange of servitude for protection. But the typical pimp never protects his slave, and allows him/her to be beaten, betrayed or even killed, responding only with ambiguous amusement."[14]

Despite the qualifications and reservations, Kate Millett sees male-female relationships as paralleling those of the homosexual world. She seems unaware of the fundamental absurdity of her proposition. For the high priestess of Women's Lib to suggest that the best way to understand the most basic human relationship is through looking at Jean Genet's exaggerated portrait of an admittedly deviant and violent homosexual world is like a theology professor claiming that we can only come to an understanding of St. Teresa or of St. John of the Cross through an exhaustive study of the activities of the frenetic nuns in Ken Russell's *The Devils.* Her theory of sexual politics may well work brilliantly for Genet-type homosexuals, but it is not valid to assume that it applies to the relationships of men and women. To "ape and exaggerate" is not necessarily to understand; it may simply be to distort and mystify. The essence of such homosexual relationships may well be uncontrolled dominance and exploitation, but we cannot assume that the average man-woman relationship shares these features. Male homosexual relationships tend to be promiscuous rather than stable and usually lack that depth of lasting affection that is the essence of stable male-female ties. Male dominance can become exploitative and callous, but not where affection is involved. It is promiscuity that may imply an asymmetrical relationship, that may involve collecting people for prestige, or the exploitation of the unattractive and the unpopular by the attractive and the desirable.

Because homosexuality is forbidden or disapproved of in many societies, it cannot be subject to regulation, to social control, in the way that the family is. The homosexual subculture exerts some control, but it cannot act openly and cannot call on the wider society for assistance. In such an unregulated world anything goes and people can seek to act out their fantasies, however destructive and extreme. Society senses this danger in deviant behavior and that is one of the reasons for prohibition in the past;

yet paradoxically this only serves to intensify the problems,[15] and further isolate the homosexual world from the mainstream of society.

The homosexual subculture may be brutal.[16] It may be true that the "male" homosexual "never protects his slave and allows him/her to be beaten, betrayed or even killed, responding only with ambiguous amusement," but would a man behave like this to the woman he loves? Would he allow another man to beat, betray or even kill his wife with impunity? Even in the most primitive societies, where the males are totally dominant, they will protect the females under any such circumstances, and they will protect them as people, not as property.[17] Because of the obsession of the Women's Libbers with the aggressive aspects of sex, it is perhaps as well to spell out the true relationship of sex to aggression and domination. A mild degree of male aggression and domination may be inferred from the nature of the sexual act itself. It is the male who must penetrate, the female who must permit. The male must be aroused or there will be no sex. There is no necessity, in this strict physical sense, for the female to be aroused—for the act of sex to occur she need only permit it. Rape is a male crime for this very reason. The female cannot rape an unwilling male; if he is unwilling, he will not be able to penetrate, or as Women's Lib would put it, he cannot be engulfed.[18] Germaine Greer quotes one Theodore Faithfull, who denies this in his epistle to the impotent: "If you ignore any idea of erection and concentrate your attention on your girl friend, ignore the clitoris and use your fingers to caress her internally and if you follow such activity by a close association of your sex organs you may soon find that she can draw your sex organ into her vagina without any need on your part for erection."[19] Germaine Greer comments: ". . . this sounds like therapeutic lying . . ."[20] It does not merely sound like it. It is, and yet another Women's Lib fantasy vanishes.

The obsession of Women's Libbers with sadomasochistic sexual aberrations stems from their belief that these aberrations are a natural extension of aggressive male sexuality. In fact, the opposite is true. Sadists tend to be precisely those men who are terrified of their own aggression, and of the aggressive aspects of male sexuality—they can only overcome this fear by deliberately and sadistically accentuating the aggressive component in all sex.[21] By suppressing the normal minor expressions of sexual aggression, the pathological ones are stimulated and encouraged. This simple point is unintentionally made by Kate Millett in her discussion of D. H. Lawrence's character Paul Morel. In *Sons and Lovers* Lawrence wrote: ". . . the nicest men he knew . . . were so sensitive to their women that they would go without them forever rather than do them a hurt. . . . They could easier deny themselves than incur any reproval from a woman . . ."[22] Millett comments: "Yet all this well-intentioned puritanism dissolves before the reader's observation of the callowness with which Paul treats both Miriam and Clara. . . . The scenes of his condescension are some of the most remarkable instances of sexual sadism disguised as masculine pedagogy which literature affords . . ."[23] Correct, but it is not his masculinity that makes Morel a sadist. Rather, it is his lack of aggressiveness, his fear of hurting a woman in bed that drives him to be cruel. Morel is a textbook "gentle sadist."

The female complement of male aggressiveness is not passivity. We do not live in "a universe of aggressions and victims."[24] Women are receptive and involved—they are neither passive victims nor inactive participants. This is not the Victorian prescription that women should "submit and endure,"[25] carefully avoiding delight; it is "tremendous surging physical ecstasy"[26] experienced "in a feminine, dynamic way."[27] Self-abandonment is a very different thing from compulsive masochism. The attempt by Women's Libbers to depict the sexual act as a symbol of the oppression of women is an inevitable extension of their preoccupation with the battle of the sexes. As soon as the relationship of the sexes is treated merely as an area for politics between two hostile parties, enjoyment is no longer possible.

The male is seen simply as an exploiting aggressor and the woman as the used, exploited victim. Under normal circumstances the dissimilarity that exists between the eroticism of men and women heightens the pleasure of both. But if these differences are seen in power terms, it becomes impossible for women to enjoy the self-abandonment that is an intrinsic element of their sexuality. The necessary precondition for women's self-abandonment is the presence of trust, tenderness and affection—all clearly absent in Germaine Greer's image of the world of sexual relationships. She carries the confrontational style of Women's Lib beyond the extremes of anyone's consciousness: "Now that sex has become political, the petty rapist had better watch his ass; he won't be getting away with it too much longer. How would you feel if a video-tape of your last fuck were playing at the Feminist Guerrilla cinema? . . . People who are fighting for their lives fight with any weapons that come to hand, so it is foolish to expect a fair fight. Sex behaviour is becoming as public as any other expression of political belief"![28] Hardly the product of close observation—lethal exaggeration has turned into blind hatred and strident jeering, reflecting an attitude that clearly makes sexual enjoyment impossible.

The current trendy insistence that the female sexual nature is identical with the male leads women compulsively to seek what they believe to be male sexual pleasures, and they are naturally disillusioned. Women's Lib has replaced the myth of the "compliant Victorian woman" with the myth of the cosmopolitan stud farm. The early Puritanical myth made it practically impossible for people, and women in particular, to communicate their real needs; in the same way, the current trendy myth of athletic, indiscriminate, sexual insatiability inhibits the communication of true feelings and desires. A deep, intimate sexual relationship is difficult to achieve in any case and such myths can only make it much harder for two people to be open to each other, unembarrassed about their relationship, tender but not soppy, forward but not strident; they lead to an unhealthy degree of introspection, and create self-conscious individuals, constantly comparing and measuring up their desires, their actions and their performance(!) against the mythical athletic model that is projected as the norm.

The Sensuous Woman was a huge best-selling success. The prescriptions for reaching "peaks of erotic pleasure you never dreamed were available to you"[29] read like something out of a contortionist's exercise book; making love in "a reclining chair," "by moonlight on the green of the twelfth hole of a golf course," "under a bed," "on top of a marble coffee table" are some of the "musts," according to its author; by the way, for the information of the not-so-trendy, making love in a swimming pool is all right but "a pretty run of the mill sport nowadays"![30] New sheets with a "leopard skin design" and lighting, "a combination of candlelight and those high intensity reading lamps"[31] are guaranteed to keep your husband or lover in the bedroom the whole weekend. Now, you may think that it would not be easy to find a man who combines the qualities of a circus contortionist with a "fine" taste for leopard-skin designed sheets—but do not despair; go on compulsively seeking him and if, when you find him, you do not reach the promised peaks of "ecstatic delight,"[32] blame your technique, your guilt complexes, your Puritanical inhibitions.

Women's Lib and *The Sensuous Woman* share a very basic attitude—they both treat woman's eroticism as identical with that of man's; *The Sensuous Woman* taking first prize for treating both of them in quite an absurd way, and Women's Lib taking first prize for branding and dismissing as a sexist anyone who dares point to fundamental differences. In fact, however, there is little doubt that woman's eroticism is much more complex, sexual excitement is much less localized, her involvement more pervasive, and the goal much more diffuse. This is not to deny the importance of the orgasm, whose nature and location in women has been the occasion of so much sterile controversy, but simply to stress the great complexity and diffusion of the female sexual experience.

There is a great deal of evidence to show that women's sexuality is distinctively different from that of men and that the differences are innate. Men are most easily sexually aroused by what they can see. Perhaps this is not surprising, since, even at the age of fourteen weeks, male infants show more interest in visual stimuli of all kinds, and unlike girls, are able to learn to respond to light signals even at this early age.[33] As a result, pornography and striptease shows exist which cater predominantly to a male audience. Women are more strongly aroused through nonvisual senses; they do respond to an erotic visual image but by projecting themselves into it, by identifying with the seductive woman in the image. It is for this reason that both men's and women's magazines are full of pictures of women. The man responds directly to them, the woman projects herself into the image. Men are more likely than women to seek casual, promiscuous affairs, and to be less dependent on longer-term emotional ties with their partners. Men are also more single-minded in their pursuit of a sexual partner and expend more energy in "search" and capture.[34] It is, of course, possible to cite men and women who are exceptions to these generalizations, but as a description of the average attitudes and behavior of men and women, they remain valid.

No doubt all these differences are interpreted by Women's Libbers as mere expressions of the sexual stereotypes imposed by society. However, girls who as fetuses were exposed to an excess of adrenal androgens (substances similar to male hormones which have a virilizing effect on the developing fetus) display typically masculine patterns of sexual behavior when adults. Even J. Money, an American researcher given to the view that sexual differences are culturally acquired (and to a singularly clumsy baroque style!), admitted that "some of these patients in adulthood have reported experiences more typically reported by normal males than females, namely erotic arousal with a strong genitopelvic component from the stimulation of visual and narrative perceptual material. Such arousal is more than the ordinary woman's arousal of romantic feeling and desire to be with her husband or boy-friend with the assuring possibility of tactile and kinaesthetic arousal. Rather it is arousal that is likely to be accompanied by . . . the willingness for sexual intercourse with even a transitory partner."[35]

Perhaps the central sexual difference between men and women is that men have greater sexual drive and women greater sexual capacity. There is a restless drive for sexual experience in men that disturbs them if they are partnerless, that drives them to seek even a casual partner. This is a direct and immediate craving often experienced by the men as a restless force that they cannot ignore and that is not found in the same way in women. Because of this quality, men rather than women indulge in sexual fantasies or bizarre perversities, read pornography and buy prostitutes. Even in Denmark, where pornography is freely sold, it is aimed at a male, not a female, market. The absence of pornography for females in such a society (though there is pornography deliberately dressed up to look as if it were meant for women but which has a male market), where there is no obliquity attached to the production and consumption of pornography, seems to indicate that women's need and enjoyment of pornography is much more limited. Women are far less aroused by pornography and in particular they are far more impervious than men to pictorial pornography.[36] This difference must be a fundamental one, or some enterprising Scandinavian entrepreneur would by now be purveying a new line in porn for women. Porn is visual. Porn is impersonal. As such it will probably remain a "men only" commodity.

For similar reasons prostitution will remain a women's profession. In the future it will neither disappear nor recruit male whores for female customers. Male prostitutes serving a female clientele are rare because women are less acutely affected by prolonged sexual abstention than men and because, whereas one female prostitute can serve a large number of male customers, a man would not last very long! Also, a woman can agree to sleep with a man even if she finds him unattractive. A male prostitute may desperately want a woman customer's money, yet be unable to perform if he finds her repellent. Perhaps Women's Lib would be happier with a bureaucratic brothel with norms and work-study productivity bonuses and time-and-motion experts. The trappings of the business world might make of prostitution a suitably nonfeminine trade. The fact that women provide prostitutes and men do not (with the single exception of male homosexual prostitutes) stems simply from these physical facts; it no longer reflects either the relative poverty of women or the self-hatred and self-denigration of the "inferior" woman in a masculine society. The women who become prostitutes in England often do so because it provides money without the usual constraints of work such as regularity, punctuality, subordination to the pace of the machine or the organization.[37] In Denmark the live-show proprietors have found that they need lesbian acts, not just because they appeal to the customer, but because they can't rely on the male partner in a heterosexual relationship being able to perform. They are similar to the men who become addicts or petty criminals because it is less demanding than regular work and has a certain false glamour. Such men would become prostitutes if they could and indeed sometimes do sell themselves to homosexuals. It is not possible to eradicate prostitution unless you can suppress the male sexual drive completely and force potential prostitutes into regular work. Only in highly unpermissive China has it been possible to achieve both these ends.[38] Everyone works for the glory of the state and Chairman Mao— the weak are driven to conform and the highly sexed to sublimate their libido in work and aggression. Prostitution has disappeared, along with the independence of the individual and sexual freedom. No one can marry at an early age, and premarital sexual experience is not allowed.[39] Are the Women's Libbers prepared to pay this price to eliminate the prostitute?

The view that man's sexual drive is stronger and more insistent than woman's is often denied by Women's Libbers despite the strong evidence in its support. They attempt to refute it by referring to sex research, such as that of Masters and Johnson, which shows in their view that "While the male's sexual potential is limited, the female's appears to be biologically nearly inexhausti-ble . . ."[40] This evidence is irrelevant. It only shows that they have confused sexual capacity and sexual drive. The existence of pros-titution, for example, depends on both the man's greater drive and the woman's greater capacity. The Women's Libbers have also confused sexual drive with sexual enjoyment and have used evidence about women's potentially greater enjoyment to infer that they have greater drive.

One index of the greater sexual drive of men is the greater incidence of bizarre sexual perversions among men than among women.[41] Women provide fewer transvestites and practically no peepers or fetishists, besides finding difficulty in exhibitionism! This seems to stem from women's lack of a restless predatory sexuality, which when repressed or diverted in men emerges in odd ways, rarely found in women.

The one form of deviation from the norm that is common among women is lesbianism. Though lesbians are not subject to the same degree of social harassment as male homosexuals, there is illustrative evidence to show that lesbians often end up being unfulfilled as women without having gained any compensating male satisfactions. Their inner confusion is often expressed in arrogance, a conspicuous exhibitionism, in an attempt to com-pensate for the femininity they have denied and the masculinity they have failed to attain. Many women become lesbians because of a natural predisposition, but for many others it is part of a general protest against the apparent antithesis of femininity and action. Women's Lib, far from solving their problem, intensifies it by provoking an open rupture between an active personality and a female sexual role. By depicting man as an adversary, they make it impossible for the disciples of Women's Lib to achieve in their sexual relationships with men the relaxation and unself-conscious "letting go" that are essential for enjoyment and fulfill-ment. The inevitable logical extension of the Women's Lib argument is that only in lesbianism can a woman attain a sexual relationship that is not belittling.[42]

For many Women's Libbers, femininity and attractiveness are the antithesis of intelligence and activity. They see the world as still being where it was when George Eliot wrote: ". . . it is the blonde and silly heroine who is in the end victorious over the more mannish brunette."[43] This view was endorsed by Simone de Beauvoir in 1949: ". . . to be feminine is to appear weak, futile, docile, the young girl is supposed not only to deck herself out, to make herself ready but also to repress her spontaneity . . . Any self-assertion will diminish her femininity and attractiveness."[44]

Such a picture of femininity may have been accurate for some social groups in Victorian England or the France of the Third Empire, but it is hardly true today. Even in the past, of course, there existed an alternative concept of what consituted feminine attractiveness. The hetaera in ancient Greece combined beauty and charm with intellect and learning. This was an idiosyncratic historical phenomenon, but it shows that even in ancient civilization, the opposition of femininity and intellect was by no means inevitable. Historically, too, the European upper-class definition of femininity contained an awareness and participation in activities extending far beyond the home. Today we can see this definition spreading to other social groups. Men's attitudes are crucial in determining how fast this change occurs, how rapidly the "new" image of femininity is adopted. Women's Libbers, far from encouraging this change, may well drive men back to the old dumb-Dora concept of what a woman should be. They continue to believe that there is an essential contradiction between "intellect" and "feminization." For Germaine Greer, "the stereotype is the Eternal Feminine . . . Her value is solely attested by the demand she excites in others. All she must contribute is her existence. She need achieve nothing, for she is the reward of achievement. She need never give positive evidence of her moral character because virtue is assumed from her loveliness, and her passivity . . .[45] Her expression must betray no hint of humor,

46

curiosity or intelligence . . ."[46] She caricatures Helene Deutsch's view of femininity by saying, "If intellect impedes feminization, intellect must go."[47] Yet she only offers us another dichotomous world in which "if feminization impedes intellect, feminization must go." Yet this antithesis is now largely kept going by the Women's Libbers' provocative discarding of their femininity to prove their intellect. They burn their bras to prove to us that they understand exothermic chemical reactions.

It is sad that they have taken this line, at the very moment when we are on the verge of establishing the new concept of the female woman which includes and incorporates intelligence and independence. Men and women can now use their differences to express what they have in common, their common intelligence and sensibility, their common interests and experiences.

What is the reaction of men to the emerging "female woman"? If Women's Lib is to be believed, men would be hostile to any interpretation of femininity which includes intelligence or independence. Whether you use the questionnaire method or study particular individuals in depth, there can be little doubt that men, far from being hostile, are enthusiastic. In a recent poll of public opinion,[48] the majority of men said that it was an advantage for a girl, in her friendships with men, to be well-educated and ambitious, and had no objection to career-minded girl friends. The survey clearly showed that the notion that attractiveness and femininity are incompatible with intelligence and independence is a notion of the past, largely irrelevant today.

Some friends with whom I discussed these findings went even further. It is worth quoting what one of them said: "The only quarrel I have with that questionnaire is that it separates attraction and intelligence at all—even conceptually. They are asking men to choose between them as if they were different things. They aren't different. They are the same thing. Intelligence is attractive—directly physically attractive. Have you met Barbara, the philosophy student? I was discussing my research with her yesterday and she took something I'd said, and analyzed it, clarified it. I suddenly saw an entirely new aspect to the problem. The effect of that on me was as if she'd taken her skirt off. It was exciting, wildly exciting. I wanted her more then than I ever had before."

The differences between men and women are the vehicle through which divergent approaches to these experiences are maintained. Far from being imprisoning stereotypes, they rescue us from a uniform conformity in which not even the difference between men and women survives. If this key difference is preserved and stressed, it makes it easier for other, more individual differences to flourish. This is all the more important when other pressures toward uniformity are so intense. As travel and technology eroded regional and cultural identity it was hoped that this would release the individual from conformity to custom and tradition and enable him to create his own world.[49] Up to a point it did, but now we seem simply to be trapped in a new, more uniform, more pervading conformity than before. Nowhere is this seen more strongly than in the United States, where the melting pot became a glue pot with individuals suffering the pains both of conformity and of uncertainty.[50]

The new concept of the female woman is so much richer and wider than the stereotype portrayed and attacked by Women's Lib that it eliminates any contradiction between femininity and intelligence. It gives ample room for the exercise of intelligent individuality while maintaining the fundamental "otherness" of men and women.

In the Women's Lib portrayal of the ideal independent woman, in its denial of femaleness, any kind of attention paid to physical appearance and attractiveness becomes a major surrender of principle. Even Germaine Greer is forced by the excesses of some "liberated" women to take a revisionist stance on this point: "It is a kind of female rebellion to eschew cosmetics and the business of attraction and some of these establishment rebels certainly cultivated respectable slatternliness to an impressive degree."[51] The problem with this type of liberated woman, as grotesque and outmoded as the dinosaur, is that they fail to realize that there is no longer any contradiction between elegance and purposeful activity. It is no longer necessary to be dripping with clumsy and fettering accessories to feel well-dressed—on the contrary, the current emphasis is on effortless and casual elegance. The attack on woman's concern with her appearance is part of a general Women's Lib attack on woman's treatment by man as a sex object. A look at newspaper supplements, both features and advertisements, shows that concern with appearance is becoming increasingly widespread among men. If the term "sex object" is to be used in this context, it has to be applied to men as well as women. But is the purpose of dressing up simply an attempt to appear a more desirable "object"? Does the Archbishop of Canterbury don his vestments to become a religious object? He is simply taking part in an accepted ritual whose meaning is emphasized by the garments he wears. The comparison is not a facetious one, for the Women's Libbers are the new sexual anabaptists who wish to extirpate ritual and color "root and branch." Soon these pleasantly suburban revolutionaries will be stabling their horses in the salons of Christian Dior. This extreme iconoclastic attitude to the ritual and romance of sex, of feeling, of belief, of life itself, is typical of the bourgeois radicals who comprise the Women's Lib movement.

Germaine Greer's attack on the monstrous regiment of unliberated women as being obsessed with "mystery, magic, champagne, ceremony, tenderness, excitement, adoration, reverence"[52] could well have come from John Knox or, come to think of it, from the Rev. Ian Paisley. Even champagne is included as a concession to the temperance movement. Perhaps she is merely rebelling against her convent background.

Like the Puritans, indeed as a promiscuous Puritan, Germaine Greer wishes to "by-pass the innuendo and short-circuit the whole process." If we try and imagine this brave new short-circuited world, bereft of all subtlety, of all ritual, of all that is not entirely functional, we are left with a world that is so drably

49

"authentic" that few would choose to live in it. If you destroy myth you do not attain truth, you merely enter a void; if you abandon ritual you do not achieve the meaning and purpose that you thought the ritual disguised and distorted. Achieving authenticity hinders rather than facilitates the ability to communicate with other people—it often destroys things you have in common. If we destroy the images we have of male and female, we do not release people—we strip them of aspects of their identity and behavior that are vital to them. We are left with "authentically" lonely and isolated individuals. Occasionally, absolute autonomy and "authentic" noncommunication is openly and unequivocally hailed as the ultimate achievement: "Sometimes one gets closer to true symbiosis if there are seven thousand miles between oneself and the other person. And then if one knows one is in at the depths of oneself, one is out of it and one cries with one's cry in one's unshared wilderness. . . .[53] Well, that sort of wilderness at least can never be possessed as anyone's territory. . . . he will remain in his desert because this is his freedom."[54]

Germaine Greer's hostility to romance stems from the false dichotomy she poses between thought and feeling. The only dependable reality for her is love as a "cognitive act,"[55] and the opposite, love as romance, is mere "swoon, possession mania."[56] All her examples of "romance" are taken from women's magazines and novelettes, from literary fantasy. People's fantasies are only a guide to their fantasies, rarely to their lives. The readers of detective stories do not tote guns around looking for criminals; the readers of science fiction do not behave like so many tentacled Martians; and in the same way, women who read *True Confessions* do not confuse these fantasies with their own real lives. For most readers, the setting of these stories is—and they know this —as remote as the dusty deserts of Mars. Germaine Greer claims that "the potency of the fantasy distorts actual behaviour,"[57] and quotes her own experience to prove it: ". . . the dream that some enormous man, say six foot six, heavily shouldered and so forth to match, will crush me to his tweeds, look down into my eyes and leave the taste of heaven or the scorch of passion on my waiting lips. For three weeks I was married to him."[58]

She fails to quote any other person who has lived out the fantasy in this way. She ought to reverse the process and turn her story into a romantic best seller with the title *For Three Scorching Weeks* or *The Taste of Heaven*. Her personal experience makes it easier to understand why she derides and ridicules so viciously the romantic myth which she regards as the centerpiece of feminine culture. Her personal animosity makes her destructive account of the romantic myth particularly entertaining. Mockery and spleen done as well as this could, of course, be used to demolish any belief or position, however worthwhile. But what alternative does she offer to those seduced by the prospect of instant "authenticity" and self-fulfillment, once the mythical stage of liberation has been achieved? She declares that women should "be deliberately promiscuous . . . and consciously refrain from establishing exclusive dependencies and other kinds of neurotic symbioses."[59] This picture of coldly chosen promiscuity and ultimate lonely isolation is so alien to woman's nature, needs and desires that it hardly needs refuting. This nature, these needs and desires are better served and better reflected in that romantic outlook which integrates thought and feeling—the outlook not of the fable, but of the women themselves.

The Family Woman

The family is the main area where the claims of emancipation diverge most strongly from the demands for liberation. Emancipation means equal status for different roles—in our present context, greater status for such distinctively female roles as wife and mother, and an extension of the freedom that the individual woman already has to define these roles according to her particular needs and outlook. Liberation is not merely a more radical extension of this; it is a demand for the abolition of wife and mother, the dissolution of the family:

> Either one goes on gradually liberating the divorce laws, until marriage stands exposed as a hollow sham in which no one would wish to engage, or one takes a short cut and abolishes marriage altogether . . .[1]

> . . . so long as every female, simply by virtue of her anatomy, is obliged, even forced, to be the sole or primary caretaker of childhood, she is prevented from being a free human being. The care of children, even from the period when their cognitive powers first emerge, is infinitely better left to the best trained practitioners of both sexes who have chosen it as a vocation, rather than to harried and all too frequently unhappy persons with little time or taste for the work of

educating minds however young or beloved. . . . the family, as that term is presently understood, must go.[2]

During the few years of their infancy we have replaced the psychologically destructive genetic parenthood of one or two arbitrary adults with a diffusion of the responsibility for physical welfare over a larger number of people.[3]

This potpourri of furious anathemas on so fundamental, so universal and so popular an institution as the family reflects the Women's Libbers' resolute determination to abolish it. What kind of empirical evidence can they produce to justify such a major break with what most women value? Where are all these wretched, exploitative families of which the wife is the most oppressed member? One answer of course is that they exist in the past, or in literature, in Victorian England (the seedier side of Victorian life is as big a favorite of the Women's Libbers as of the pop historians of pornography), or feudal France, in the acutely described but hardly representative families created by Strindberg or Albee.

The only real, live, still-in-existence families that they ever refer to are their own. Memories of the author's unhappy childhood are trotted out to prove that the family is rotten to the core. The argument runs roughly: I am unhappy because I had an unhappy childhood. My childhood took place in a family. Therefore families are a bad thing. Because I am what my childhood made me, I am unlikely ever to be happily married. Therefore marriage is a bad thing.

Germaine Greer's childhood recollections aptly make this point:

My father had decided fairly early on that life at home was pretty unbearable; and he lived more and more of it at his club, only coming home to sleep. My mother did not protest about this as it gave her an opportunity to tyrannize the children and enlist their aid to disenfranchise my father completely . . . The most sinister aspect of domestic infighting is the use of the children as weaponry and battlefield. . . . my mother used to mutter to me that my father was a "senile old goat." . . . Once my mother knelt on my small brother's chest and beat his face with her fists in front of my father and was threatened with violent retaliation, the only instance of my father's rising to the bait that I can recall. My brother was three years old at the time.[4]

Life with the Greers is hardly typical. It is quite understandable that her childhood experience should color her view of the family in general. It is even fair to use the pathological to understand the normal; aspects of normal life can be seen there in an exaggerated form and sometimes they are made clearer by the exaggeration. But it is invalid to imply that the normal is identical with the pathological or that because they have common elements they are therefore both evil, or even that the elements they have in common but in different amounts must be eradicated. High blood pressure is dangerous, but the answer is not to eliminate blood pressure altogether.

At least, however, Germaine Greer has chosen to focus on marriage as a means of individual fulfillment rather than first as a social institution. The crucial issue is not the venerable institution of matrimony but the man-woman relationship. It is an inner compulsion that today leads us into this man-woman relationship rather than the external demands of society, rather than economic necessity or pressure from one's relatives as in a Greek village, or even a big Greek "village" like Athens. The Women's Libbers come from societies where the freedom to choose whether, when and whom to marry is so established that they take it completely for granted. From the vantage point of a traditionalist country like Greece, their protests against the far looser and more subtle pressures of Western societies seem hollow and misplaced. They seem to be shouting for freedom, when they are free already. In fact, of all the freedoms that in Western societies are taken as basic, as axiomatic, there is none more unquestionable than the freedom to choose the person you wish to marry.

The close link between marriage and the romantic idea of

falling in love imposes, of course, far greater demands on the man-woman relationship in marriage. Men and women are no longer content with an impersonal legal contractual arrangement. What they want is a constantly developing love affair in marriage.

There is a certain irony in the Women's Lib demand for the marriage relationship to be made once again an impersonal contractual matter. What they will create, if they succeed, is a more egalitarian and certainly more transitory version of the rural Greek marriage, where a dowry contract is drawn between the two parties and the division of labor within the family is firmly and rigidly defined. Not as rigidly, however, as by a contract signed recently by a "liberated" New York couple: "Sub-section (b): Housework; Clause 8, Cooking: Breakfasts during the week divided equally; husband does all weekend breakfasts (including shopping for them, and dishes afterwards). Wife does all dinners except Sunday nights; husband does . . ."![5]

The view of marriage implied in such contracts, drawn by trendy, "liberated" people, is in fact the most reactionary and outdated view possible. It shifts the basis of marriage away from the fulfillment of the needs for companionship and intimacy, away from the concept of a "growing love affair," away from personal solutions and answers to personally perceived problems, and back to the necessary but definitely auxiliary tasks of doing the dishes, making the beds and doing the shopping.

Demosthenes said of Athenian women that "we have hetaeras for the pleasures of the spirit, concubines for sensual pleasures, and wives to give us sons."[6] Modern woman is expected to be all three to her husband—there is no doubt that the conception of the man-woman relationship in marriage has never been as complex and ambitious. When marriage is merely the state of not being divorced and when most pleasures—sexual and mental—are sought outside it, it is hardly surprising that, legally, marriage failures are few. When, however, the expectation is that marriage will meet all the personality needs of the two partners—and the establishment of a home and the bringing up of children are only a part of these needs—then a greater number of marriage failures is one of the inevitable results of a much richer, infinitely more fulfilling and undisputably harder concept of marriage. The man-woman relationship is the most personal, deepest and potentially most beautiful relationship two human beings can have. The fact that the Western view of marriage has recognized this, and has made this relationship rather than the procreative or social function of marriage the central one, is a very marked advance on the position in a traditionalist country like Greece today or England in the past.

No single relationship between two people, however perfect, can completely fulfill *all* the facets of both personalities. To expect absolute fulfillment from a claustrophobic version of *égoisme à deux* is to carry the new, high concept of marriage to an extreme so unrealistic that it has disillusionment built into it. It is an attempt to live out in reality Aristophanes' Androgynous[7]—the complete fusion of two complementary parts that had been frantically wandering the earth looking for each other. It is a myth that describes a real need, an actual, almost compulsive drawing of a man to a woman, but the fanciful ending of fusion is foolishly misleading. If a couple tries to attain this state, at worst the relationship dies of suffocation, and at best it has very limiting effects on both of them; it implies an opting out of the rest of the world and a false assumption that their relationship has reached a perfect, static harmony and that no more effort or development is needed. The "planetary law of distance" in the relation of people to one another has an astronomical loneliness about it, but is valuable if only because it stresses the dangers of fusion as well as distance. "For some of the circle of one's acquaintances, it may be said that one loves them cordially at a hundred miles' distance; of others that they are dear friends at a mile; while others again are indispensable far nearer than that. If by any chance the friend whose planetary distance is a mile is forced into close quarters, the only result is a violent development of repulsion and centrifugal force, by which probably he is carried even beyond his normal distance, till such time as he settles down into his right place"![8]

A relationship between two people, however, is not just a question of how far they are apart or how close they are together; it is also a result of what the people themselves are like. The combination may be greater than the sum of the parts, but there are limits to the extent to which a human institution can transcend the limitations of the participants. Two limited individuals will have a limited relationship. It may not be as limited as they are, but it will be limited nonetheless. Criticisms of the institution that hinge on the citing of such examples fail to see that success or failure of an institution like marriage is often intrinsic to the nature of the individuals involved. The modern tendency to treat all people as a homogeneous mass, and to be extremely wary of stressing individual differences, has meant that marriages that are flat, uninspired and unfulfilling have been used as proof that marriage has failed as an institution. The truth is that, however untrendy this may sound, some people are boring and some are nasty and whatever relationships they enter into will share these characteristics. Whatever social arrangements we invent on which to build the man-woman relationship, and however ingenious they are, there will be those who find this mutual involvement stultifying.

The greater stress on the man-woman relationship within marriage has not, in most cases, detracted from the importance of the relationship between mother and child. The creativity of maternity and the joys of motherhood have been dwelt on so strongly and for so long that it is difficult to discuss them without blundering into somebody else's clichés. Here the iconoclasts have a long start over the traditionalists and can easily provide euthanasia for dying metaphors and images; images that have lost their freshness and metaphors deprived of their vividness can persuasively be made to look as if they have lost their meaning as well. The universality of motherhood has helped the Women's Libbers in their campaign to label it a mundane experience. The feelings of women who, for a considerable part of their lives thought themselves unable to have children, are a better guide and a useful reminder for other women of how important maternity is. Even Nemone Lethbridge, a supporter of Women's Lib, wrote:

> Three months later I was pregnant. Not *perhaps*—pregnant, not *hope*—I'm pregnant, but actually, gloriously, clinically provenly, pregnant. The pathologist telephoned me: Are you pleased or disappointed? Pleased? I could jump over the moon. I've waited eleven years for this. Well, mind you hold on to it then. Congratulations. It was the middle of June. The garden was dark with leaves; the ground underfoot was pink where the chestnuts had cast their blossoms. I hugged myself again and again. Beowulf, my dog, who thought I had gone stark staring crazy, butted me in the back of the knees because I kept forgetting to throw the ball for him. Hold on to it? I'll hold on to it if it kills me. Atalanta. Aurelian. It would have made no difference even if I had known exactly what this pregnancy was going to mean: seven months in hospital, the loss of all the work I'd so patiently collected for myself, the bleeds, the false alarms, the pethidene, the Caesarian section with its sequential sense of alienation, the baby blues.[9]

Bearing and giving birth to a child is an experience not comparable to any other. At no other time is a human being so near to creation, so near to affirming life and glimpsing immortality. A long way away from Kate Millett's "simply by virtue of her anatomy . . . prevented from being a free human being."[10] Do women really see motherhood in this way? Or does it provide a role which largely releases them from the existential anxieties of today; from the pervasive problem of meaninglessness that increasingly overrides the problem of frustration? What am I here for? What is it that I want out of life? How can I use my freedom? The woman has an answer in her baby. The existence of this answer does not preclude the search for alternatives; it simply provides one answer that is not and could never be available to men. Women are never excluded from men's answers in this same immutable way. The difference between emancipation and liberation is particularly stark here. Emancipation is free access for women to all alternative or sequential answers, all regions of human experience. Liberation is the denial of any intrinsic value to maternity and, if necessary, the replacement of mother by the machine. Shulamith Firestone, who describes pregnancy as "barbaric," "shitting a pumpkin" or "the temporary deformation of the body of the individual for the sake of the species,"[11] proclaims that "artificial methods will have to be developed hurriedly, or at the very least satisfactory compensations [for women]—other than destructive ego investments—would have to be supplied to make it worth their while."[12]

Assuming Miss Firestone does not get away with her machines, women who have children will want to be identified with them and keep them with them. Child care, according to the Libbers, is "culturally assigned to women."[13] It is conceivable that a society could exist where women handed the children over to men the minute they were born. But who is more likely to be most strongly emotionally oriented to baby feeding and child rearing —the woman for whom the child has been a part of herself for nine months or the man whose role is relatively peripheral? The woman is, after all, physically designed to feed the child for some time after birth—the man needs the help of bottles and sterilized teats! Does it not make more sense to build on the strong emotional bond of mother and child, established by pregnancy and feeding, rather than to start from scratch? The fact that the pattern of child care by women has been culturally reinforced does not render it any the less natural. Any alternative social pattern would not merely have to be culturally reinforced—it would have to be culturally created, with no biological basis on which to build and develop.

Kate Millett typifies the Women's Lib attitude by claiming that woman "is obliged, even forced, to be the sole or primary caretaker of childhood."[14] No woman is obliged or forced to have a child, and most women who do have children do so *because* they want to bring them up. For those "liberated" women who do not wish to have anything to do with bringing up their children, there is a simple solution: don't have any. The social pressures on women to marry and have children are much more easily withstood than the Women's Libbers allege. They write as if the First World War had never taken place and society's expectations of women were still Edwardian. In England, the First World War killed a million actual and potential husbands and fathers, and after the war, and ever since, it has become normal and acceptable to lead a life that does not involve being a mother. In typical Women's Lib fashion, once it is established that the evidence does not back up their claim that people are pushed by networks of relatives and associates into getting married, they proceed to argue exactly the opposite and claim that this proves their case equally well. They have taken up the position of the man who was reckless enough to attack the Good Soldier Schweik. He had mistaken Schweik for someone else and when he noticed his error, he was so angry that he attacked Schweik even harder. Nobody likes being wrong.[15] In the same fashion, in the absence of moral pressures toward marriage, the Women's Libbers have discovered or invented a new set of social forces pressing the single woman irresistibly into marriage and childbirth against her will and against her better judgment. "Today those who do not marry and have children by a certain age are penalized: they find themselves alone, excluded and miserable on the margins of a society in which everyone else is compartmentalized into lifetime generational families, chauvinism and exclusiveness their chief characteristics."[16] This is not the experience of most people who choose to remain single. The middle-class intellectuals of Manhattan held up by Miss Firestone as models of how to live a single life may have lost contact with their relatives, but for a lot of people, kinship ties remain very important. "Chauvinistic" though it may be, people continue to value their brothers, sisters, cousins and nephews. The authority of the extended family has disappeared, but the ties remain.[17] Relatives have become "as-

criptive friends." Single people are not excluded by the "chauvinism" of other people's families unless, of course, they insist on
subjecting the family to destructive and often personal abuse
based on the ideological prejudices of Women's Lib. Single people, through their married friends, are assured both of adult
companionship and of contact with children. Families, far from
being "chauvinistic" about their children, in the sense of exclud-
ing them from contact with other people, are proud of them and
enjoy their friends playing and talking with them. Most people,
if they go back to their childhood, remember the important part
played in it by uncles and aunts, married or unmarried, real or
adopted from friends of the family.

The evidence is overwhelmingly against the view that life for
the single individual is inevitably a lonely and isolated one. It is
not, then, the fear of a miserable alternative that pushes people
into marriage, but a positive desire for the distinctive intimacy
that marriage can bring. It is not even the desire for casual contact with children but the much more positive wish to have and
bring up children of one's own. Kate Millett's view that "The care
of children . . . is infinitely better left to the best trained practi-
tioners of both sexes who have chosen it as a vocation"[18] shows
a total lack of insight into parents' feelings toward their children.
Millett sees the role of "mother" as a sort of child-care officer.
There is a difference between a vocation for child care and a
desire to bring up and care for one's own children. Emotionally,
the two roles make very different demands and bring very different satisfactions. This sounds like a plea for what the Libbers call
family chauvinism[19] (chauvinism—any form of emotional attachment that Women's Libbers do not share). For the really liberated woman, the love of the mother for her child is antisocial
because it differentiates that child from all other children. In Miss
Greer's Utopian fantasy, set in a Mediterranean farmhouse, she
proudly proclaims that "the child need not even know that I was
his womb-mother."[20]

The theory behind this is that we would love humanity the

more if we ceased to love certain individuals so intensely. The moral reformers of the past have always stressed the need to extend family love beyond the confines of the family. The very language of morality confirms this. The Brotherhood of Man; *Liberté, Egalité, Fraternité;* even, in the words of Lord George-Brown, "Brothers!"; but Women's Lib claims not merely to be "pushing the frontiers" but to be breaking down the very barriers that limit the numbers and kind of people to whom we extend our involvement and a sense of moral obligation. We must allow love "to flow unimpeded."[21] In practice, they are urging a moral implosion where the indifference that we all too often feel toward strangers is to be extended into the heart of the family. Extension of total indifference inward, rather than extension of family involvement outward, is the likely result of the Women's Liberation campaign.

Women's Liberation here displays a certain congruence with other groups of "liberated" people, who characteristically fail to be capable of the deep and consistent feelings that all personal relationships demand, and yet proclaim a diffuse love of humanity. They are an inverted version of Dean Swift: they love humanity and cannot abide Tom, Dick or Harry;[22] they hate people and love mankind. They are guilty of one of the great moral fallacies of our time—the belief that, somehow, a collective paradise can be pursued and achieved, irrespective of personal behavior. Whenever anyone is treated spitefully or callously by a "liberated" person, the defense of his "comrades in liberation" will always be: "But you can't judge him by ordinary standards." It would seem that we must apply special standards of meanness, selfishness and vindictiveness to the "liberated"; the standards expected of them are lower. There is a kind of nihilism about the "liberated." Their general attitude is that all moral issues will effortlessly disappear once the collective mystic state of liberation has been achieved: I am contributing to the success of the venture of Liberation—that is my debt to humanity paid. I need not bother to behave morally in other ways, and in any case these ways are about to disappear.

Many Women's Libbers talk as if the state of liberation were to be achieved effortlessly, painlessly and immediately. Germaine Greer swings recklessly from the manic fantasy that "it might be possible to leap the steps of revolution and arrive somehow at liberty and communism without strategy or revolutionary discipline."[23] On another occasion, with an amazing burst of common sense, she admitted that there would be at least three generations of a chaotic transitional period before the promised land was entered—a transitional period characterized by harshness and suffering.[24] It is clear from the wild millenarian statements which she makes that she is unwilling to even begin to think quantitatively about the issues and is unable to see past, present and future in an integrated way.[25] We are offered definite hardships now, and ill-defined and uncertain benefits the-day-after-the-day-after-tomorrow. There is, of course, risk involved in any major social change and there are gambles which have to be taken. But in the package offered by Women's Liberation, the anguish is more certain and the gains more distant and more illusory than any revolutionary has ever had the impudence to offer before. It is fair to ask men and women to set the world on its head to gain a bowl of rice a day where there was no bowl before; you can hardly ask them to do it to assuage the unrepresentative discontents of a noisy intellectual minority.

Who would bear the transitional costs? The first victims of the disruption that would follow a mass abandonment of relationships and responsibility for the pursuit of a miasmic and strictly egocentric individuality would be the children. This has been glibly passed over by the Women's Libbers, whose exclusive preoccupation seems to be the abolition—rather than the viable replacement—of the family. Pie in the sky replaces pie in the oven.

Shulamith Firestone advocates "households" with a "limited

contract" consisting of a number of adults and children in a loose and voluntary association. Some restriction on the transfer of adults, though not children, in and out of the group is envisaged, but the problems created by a high turnover are never really faced. We are taught that "the child would still form intimate relationships but instead of developing close ties with a decreed 'mother' and 'father,' the child might now form these ties with people of its own choosing, of whatever age or sex."[26] This is typical of the Women's Lib obsession with children's "rights." Millett urges "the end of the present chattel status and denial of rights to minors."[27] This is good rousing stuff for the seventeen-year-old, but what about the two-year-old? Does he want his rights—to do as he wishes, to look after himself? Does he even know what he wants? Is it rights he wants or the parents' love and tenderness? David Cooper, in urging "the death of the family," shows the same symptoms of bitterness and hatred, completely blotting out common sense; he paints horror pictures of what happens "if one does not discover one's autonomy in one's first year of life," and ends with this piece of faultlessly liberated logic: "In any case one has to leave home one day. May be the sooner the better"![28] An adult's first right is to be free, but despite all the pearls of commune-span wisdom and all admonitions that we are "victims of a surfeit of security,"[29] a child's first right *continues* to be security and affection. Here we see, in extreme form, Millett's inability to realize that a relationship that is less than fully egalitarian can be a source of joy to both parties and does not have to be exploitative. Most mothers cannot be said, in any meaningful sense, to exploit a small child, and the satisfaction that a mother derives from loving her child is hardly an exploiting satisfaction or even a purely selfish one.

Under Shulamith Firestone's system, the small child's right to security and affection is sacrificed in order to provide him with the right to pack up his toys in a case and go off to find a new, strange "household." Even if the child "chooses" to stay where he is, the adults may choose to move. Either a particular adult, when he/she moves, takes a particular child with him/her, in which case a familial tie of dependence is restored, or else we have a rapid turnover of the adults of the household which would give it all the characteristics of a badly run orphanage.

In another Women's Lib Utopia, "adult child relationships would develop just as do the best relationships today; some adults might prefer certain children over others, just as some children might prefer certain adults over others"![30] This is supposed to be an ideal egalitarian community, but there is nothing as inegalitarian as popularity. Although families may be "unequal," each child has a particular mother and father who love it because it is their own, even if the child next door is cleverer, prettier and more appealing. In a communal environment with no fixed ties, the most attractive children are likely to get all the adult affection and attention, while the unattractive child enjoys his inalienable human "right" to loneliness and neglect. Calvin wanted to turn the world into a monastery;[31] Women's Lib wants to turn it into an orphanage.

Germaine Greer rather finds her Utopia in the stem family of feudal times. "Family problems could be challenged openly in the family forum and the decisions of the elders were honoured. Romantic love as a motive for cohabitation was hardly important. A man only needed to desire to breed by a woman who would fit in with his household. Disappointment, resentment and boredom had less scope. The children benefited by the arrangement and in parts of Greece and Spain and Southern Italy still do . . . When I lived in a tiny hamlet in Southern Italy I saw such a family bravely holding together in spite of the grimmest poverty and the absence of most of the men, who were working in Germany, and their children were the happiest, the least coy and irritable of any that I have ever observed."[32] The importance of this distorted description of southern Italy, Greece or Spain is that it provides the basis for Germaine Greer's dream of what might replace the nuclear family: "For some time now, I have pondered the problem of having a child which would not suffer from my neuroses and the difficulties I would have in adjusting to a husband and the demands of domesticity. . . . I thought again of the children I knew in Calabria and hit upon the plan to buy, with the help of some friends with similar problems, a farmhouse in Italy where we could stay when circumstances permitted, and where our children would be born. The fathers and other people would also visit the house as often as they could, to rest and enjoy the children and even work a bit."[33] Germaine Greer's household would fail for the same reasons as Shulamith Firestone's. She says of the "rambling organic structure of my *ersatz* household" that it is "an unbreakable house in that it does not rest on the frail shoulders of two bewildered individuals . . ."[34] But on whose shoulders does it rest? Who looks after the children when no one wants to, who puts up the cash if everyone wishes to be idle, who remains with the children if everyone wants to leave the household? There is no reason why separate, nuclear families should not collaborate in setting up a shared household, provided it is realized who is responsible for what—that is, provided that the structure of the family and its psychological and economic responsibilities are retained. This preserves and buttresses the family. It is hardly liberation.

Germaine Greer's "plan" for replacing the family is even more ludicrous because it hinges on a description of the extended family that has only the most tenuous link with reality. I have spent a somewhat larger part of my life than Miss Greer in a country where the Mediterranean extended family is still prevalent and I can say that when, in Germaine Greer's words, the decisions of the elders are honored, family problems are in fact settled by the favoritism of the senile. Decisions are honored only because they are imposed by an authority which, though unchallenged, is often resented. Where "romantic love" is absent as "a motive for cohabitation," a girl is given away in marriage to a man who is only the best husband for her in the sense that he is the best husband her dowry can buy. A man does not marry a woman; he marries an olive grove, or an oil tanker, a certificate of virginity, or a guarantee of fertility—meaning sons! Even if the wife loves her husband, this may simply mean that her life within the extended family is even more frustrating. Pirandello, who again saw more of family life in southern Italy than Germaine Greer, wrote a story, "The Cooper's Cockerels," about the fate of the wife in such a family setup. "The wife of Marchica, the Cooper, had one overwhelming desire: to be allowed—just once, at least! —to have her Christmas dinner alone with her husband, or dinner on Easter Sunday, for that matter, or on New Year's Day, or at Carnival time. No, whatever the festive occasion, it was his custom to gather round his table hordes of relatives and friends. Very much to his wife's regret."[35]

"Disappointment, resentment and boredom have less scope" only in the sense that they are effectively repressed. Sometimes they burst out in fits of quasi-religious hysteria—when all the disappointment, boredom and resentment that Germaine Greer failed to notice are expressed in melodramatic defiance of the woman's husband and kin.[36] As for the bucolic idealization of rural poverty where the children are "the happiest, the least coy and irritable" of all the children that Germaine Greer has "ever observed," it sounds too much like Marie Antoinette's view of the happy milkmaids. What is frightening about this idealized picture of family life in southern Italy is the hatred it reveals. Germaine Greer's irrational hatred of the nuclear family is so extreme that it leads her to glorify any potential alternative, however wretched the reality.

At the other extreme of Germaine Greer's "organic" sogginess lies the arid, mechanical views of Kate Millett. For Kate Millett, among the chief defects of the nuclear family is that it is "a wasteful and inefficient body" noted for its "unsystematic and individualistic manner" of work.[37] Clearly, Miss Millett would like the family to be turned into a bureaucracy, with personal relations so basic to the family, characterized by efficiency, systematic planning and uniformity. Only somebody who sees the family as an exercise in sexual politics comparable with party politics, or corporation politics, and is blind to the fact that the essence of the family is relationships, would want to remodel it along the lines of General Motors or the Trans-Siberian Railway.

We should not judge the Women's Libbers too harshly for advocating alternatives to the family which can immediately be seen to be ludicrous, when all the probable alternatives have been tried and found wanting. Historically there have been occasions when the abolition of the family was one of the aims of a revolutionary party coming to power. In the Soviet Union, a serious attempt was made to abolish the family and to render women and children economically independent of men. It was the intention of the revolutionaries to set up state nurseries to take the care of the children out of the hands of the mothers, and to establish collective housekeeping to free women from household chores, but the social chaos caused by the undermining of the family in these early years, especially a great upsurge of violent hooliganism among the neglected children, forced the Soviet government to reverse its policy. Women's Libbers are acutely uncomfortable about the implications of the Soviet experience and try to explain away the failure of this attempt to abolish the family by rather far-fetched special pleading. Their favorite "excuse" is that the Russians were not prepared to face the economic costs to society involved in such a drastic change.[38] If these costs were so large as to daunt a revolutionary government which had no qualms about taking the nation to the verge of starvation by its doctrinaire persecution of the kulaks, then it is difficult to see why any society should ever be willing to suffer them. In any case, although since that time the Russians have created a wealthy industrial economy, they have shown no signs of reverting to their earlier policy of destroying the family.

Another piece of special pleading was that the psychological difficulties of making a change to a new system were too great to be borne.[39] If the psychological difficulties were too great to be borne then, why should it be supposed that they will be more easily borne now? The Russians can hardly be criticized for timidity; they ruthlessly pushed through other social changes demanding a significant alteration in people's psychological outlook. Private property was abolished, religion dethroned and a backward, feudal country rapidly industrialized. Even the family itself did not remain unaltered, for the rambling, patriarchal, extended family was replaced by the nuclear family—a change that demanded an entirely new set of attitudes and patterns of behavior. At a time when every social institution and established attitude was transformed or even turned on its head, it is absurd to claim that it was caution or timidity that restrained the revolutionaries from abolishing the family altogether.

Any credibility that the special pleading arguments about Russia retained has been dissipated by the failure of subsequent, and in some ways more drastic, revolutions to abolish the family. Germaine Greer sadly admits that the revolution in China "did not entail any amelioration of the woman's role as servant of her family,"[40] and after the revolution in Cuba, "Fidel Castro besought them [women] to return to their former menial roles."[41] Despite Germaine Greer's loaded terminology, one thing is clear —socialist revolutions do not involve the disappearance of the family.

Another revolutionary regime which, for ideological reasons, wanted to abolish the family was that of the Nazis in Germany. The Nazis are often described by those sympathetic to Women's Lib as upholders of the German familial tradition. The truth is that the party ideologues saw the ultimate National Socialist society as one in which the family had ceased to exist, but because of the strength of German public opinion in favor of the family, they were forced to appear publicly as its upholders so as to gain power. The Nazis were strongly influenced by the German sociologist Hans Blüher, who advocated the replacement of the family by segregated male communities (*Ordensburgen*).[42] They did, in fact, establish *Ordensburgen* in monasteries and convents seized from the Roman Catholic Church, and this is where the Nazi élite was supposed to be brought up and trained for leadership.[43] These communities were to replace the family as the foundation on which the state was to rest; the family as a constituent cell in society would be abolished while women would be relegated to "a purely animal function."[44] Blüher was as strong an enemy of the family as any Women's Libber. He declared: ". . . where the family takes a prominent place in life, there the mind stagnates. Under the family regime, tradition dominates; where the male community rules, the revolutionary spirit prevails . . . If there were only the family as the basis of the human social systems, nothing more would be achieved beyond the maintenance of the species."[45]

Blüher's view of the family as a purely animal institution has the same ring of irrationality about it as the rantings of Women's Lib. In fact, the Nazi slogan "Woman is man's deadly enemy" could easily be turned around and used by Women's Lib. The form would be different but the message would be the same—the relationship between man and woman is seen as one of political conflict and confrontation. Both the Nazi ideologues and Women's Lib are so obsessed with the notion of dominance that they are unable to see the two sexes as different but complementary; they can only see them in terms of inferiority and superiority. The distinctive identity of women is despised both by the Nazis and by Women's Lib. Samuel Igra sums up the Nazi attitude: "When Blüher says that woman is man's deadly enemy he means and expounds his theory at great length that humanity has hitherto failed to achieve and maintain itself on a heroic level, because men have allowed themselves to succumb to the virtues of human kindness, sympathy and charity which are characteristic of the feminine sex. The reason for this is that men have identified the romantic love element—the *eros* as Blüher calls it—with the intermingling of the sexes in procreative and family life. Love between men and women, mutual affection between parents and children, especially the mother's love for her child—all these are the expression of the same procreative instinct which man has in common with the animals."[46]

Blüher, like Women's Lib, despises motherhood and femininity. Women's Lib sees these roles as degrading and wants women to abandon them; Blüher sees them as degrading and wants to isolate men from their corrupting influence. Neither he nor Women's Lib is able to understand the value of the distinctively female virtues and activities. Only the masculine aspects of life are worth having, worth preserving and fostering. Women are either to be turned into men, or else remain women and be despised by supermales. They are not allowed to be themselves, to be respected for what they are. Women's Lib sees the family as a means by which men oppress women, the Nazis saw it as a trick by women to oppress men. Professor Alfred Baumler, the director of the Political Department at the University of Berlin under the Nazis, saw the family as the basis of an effete urban order: "Within this kind of civilization the man plays a secondary part. In this system the woman dominates as the ruler and misleader of man."[47] All the prejudices of the Nazis were bound up with this hatred for family life. The Jews were attacked by Blüher as suffering from a "morbid enlargement of the family idea"; Baumler attacked the Social Democrats for "having promoted family life and taught the youth to respect their parents and look to family training as the source of their guiding ideals in life."[48] The family was even accused of taking part in the "stab in the back" that lost Germany the First World War. In *Mein Kampf* Hitler accused the wives of Germany of having destroyed the morale of the soldiers at the front by writing letters to them about the shortage of food and the sufferings of their families, reminding them of family life and sapping the determination of the army to fight on.[49] Through the family, the women had destroyed the men.

Both the Nazis and Women's Lib see the family as a political battleground, and both despise the distinctively female virtues that the family epitomizes. In the Nazi ideology, only men are to become supermen; for Women's Lib this should be the goal of women as well. Not merely are the goals similar but also some of the means, for the superman—male or female—is to emerge from the struggle between men and women, from a ruthless form of sexual politics. The Nazis saw the family as sapping the virile qualities of men; Women's Lib sees it as preventing women from attaining these same qualities.

A happier, more democratic attempt to replace the family was the kibbutz experiment in Israel. In the kibbutz, most of the formal institutional demands of Women's Lib have been met. The social pressures which structure woman's role in other societies have been removed. There is full economic equality, all women have jobs and are no longer economically dependent on men. The development of institutions for the care of children has resolved the conflicting demands of job and family. Women are expected to play a full part in the political, economic and social life of the kibbutz. Household chores—cooking, laundry, mending—have been collectivized and are performed by a professional kibbutz staff. Despite all these drastic changes, the family has stubbornly refused to wither away and the distinctive roles of men and women have not been eliminated. Women were offered liberation and settled for emancipation. In the early days of the kibbutz "women's striving was towards identification with men, towards an equality that disregarded sex differences and that set forth male qualities and activities as the model for both sexes."[50] In such a society, prestige only went to those involved in purely masculine occupations, such as heavy agricultural work. A few women who were suited by personality or physique to these tasks had the respect of the whole community, but it was the other women who paid the price for this. The areas in which they excelled, such as child care or service occupations, were allocated a very low rank by the community's ideology, which meant that women were forced to compete for status and esteem in areas where nature had loaded the dice heavily in favor of men. Ironically, the position of most individual women was lower than it would have been if the ideology of liberation from sex roles had not existed. The ideology of the kibbutzim was forced to alter its aims from liberation to emancipation; from "the former male oriented and mechanical interpretation of women's equality" to "a recognition of differences in the interests and capacities of men and women—differences that in no way render women inferior to men";[51] from women as orange pickers in the merciless skin-drying Middle Eastern sun to women as beauticians and part-time beauty "objects."

All these changes were related to parallel changes in the family. The founding mothers of the kibbutzim were deeply suspicious of the family, strongly rejecting the family life they had known in Europe. The role of the family in the community was minimized and many saw this as a stepping stone to the complete abolition of the family. Over the years, though, the kibbutzim did not make a great stride forward to the next stepping stone—or more accurately a plunge into the water searching for a stepping stone that does not exist. Rather, they almost unconsciously turned around and took a few sleepwalking steps back toward the family. Parents were allowed to play a larger part in bringing up their children —in some kibbutzim even, children were allowed to sleep in their parents' rooms. The greater importance of marriage and the family is symbolized in the changes in marriage ceremonies within the kibbutz. In the early days, marriage was a small, cultural, informal event, and few guests attended such an unimportant occasion. Now there are special and elaborate marriage ceremonies, enormous festive celebrations involving the whole of the kibbutz and guests from outside. Women in the kibbutzim are now marrying at a much earlier age, even though this means that they have to abandon their plans for higher educational and vocational training outside the kibbutz. What is particularly significant is that they should choose to behave in this way in the absence of moral and economic pressures to get married and despite the presence of a strong work ethic that stresses the importance of vocational training and "self-realization through work" for both men and women. Menachem Gerson sums up the situation in the kibbutz today: "Young women rejoining the kibbutz after army service wish to begin as early as possible to build their family nests . . . Job involvement seems to be weaker among young women in the kibbutz than are family considerations; when job and family conflict preference is given to the latter, as indicated by the trend to earlier marriage."[52]

On Women's Lib assumptions, it would be expected that the women had fought uncapped tooth and unmanicured nail against the changes imposed by male chauvinists. The truth is that women, not men, have been most prominent in urging a greater role for the family within the kibbutz and increased contact between parents and children. Insofar as women see the kibbutz as oppressive, it is not because they are excluded from masculine pursuits but rather because they are prevented from fully following female ones. As Dr. Rivka Bar-Yosef, a woman sociologist from the Hebrew University, put it: "The whole concept of male chauvinism seems passé in Israeli terms . . . now women want to be feminine."[53]

The desire to be female in a rigidly egalitarian society can lead to personal tragedy. Young mothers have been forced to leave, or threatened with expulsion, because they refused to leave their babies in the children's home overnight. One mother who was, in fact, a leading educator in her kibbutz, described her feelings when she had to part from her two-week-old baby in terms that are moving to all but those who despise maternity: "During these two weeks I became very attached to my baby and when the time came for him to go to the infants' house, I felt terrible . . . I cried for a week; I was very unhappy. I used to run to the infants' house as often as I could to see if the child was all right. At the time I wasn't allowed to enter when I wanted; I had to try to look through the window."[54] Other mothers, more resolute, persuaded their husbands, despite their objections, to leave the kibbutz so that their children could live with them. The aim of the kibbutz is to end, from the start, the attachment that has developed with the mother feeling the baby growing inside her for nine months, and to distance the mother from the child very early on. It is only this objective that can explain why babies are not allowed into their parents' rooms for the first six months. Later the children will spend two hours a day in the parents' room, but as Bruno Bettelheim put it, "a place that offers the kind of security that stops by the hand of the clock merely rubs in how precarious a haven it is[55]. . . What is natural—the mother's breast and her milk—she is ready and able to give. But when the giving could grow into a unique one-to-one relationship it is restricted in time and meaning. Otherwise it might interfere with the mother's collective relations or even with the infant's relating to the peer group[56]. . . Parents and children are aware that limits exist, and if they were not aware and exceeded them the *metapelet* would step in . . . and soon it will be clear to the child that his parents are basically daily and sabbath visitors in his life, and he in theirs."[57] The inevitable result of this attitude is that parents and children are unable to have a relaxed relationship; every day, when saying goodbye to each other, they have to repress their feelings and their attachment. To protect themselves from the pains of regular, communally enforced separation, they become wary of ever letting this attachment develop into a deep relationship.

The guilt the parents feel about loving their children "too strongly" is curiously similar to the guilt some Victorians felt about sexual passion. The effect of continuous repression is to stultify the emotional life both of the Victorian and of the progressive Puritans. This repression has an even more mutilating effect on the child's emotional development. A man who left the kibbutz explained why, in terms of these psychological effects of kibbutz upbringing: "He felt that the pervasive, though benevolent control of the kibbutz had muted his personality; that it kept him from experiencing not only his own passions but also his own weaknesses, because the kibbutz always protected him from the consequences. It had denied him the right to experience his own grief and his own joys. Since the community decided what his actions should be in most matters that count, often acted for him in fact, he could never feel it was he who had done the right thing. He wanted the privilege of feeling all this, even of doing wrong if he had to."[58] If the child's life is totally regulated by the collective, if he has no time of his own, no place where he can be on his own and one-to-one intimacy is heavily discouraged, it becomes inevitable that throughout his life he will be completely incapable of forming deep personal relationships or of functioning effectively away from the group.

The flat personality, the shallow emotions, the fear of intimacy, the compulsive conformity and group loyalty of the average kibbutznik are strikingly similar to the character traits of the worst products of the English public (i.e., private) schools. Boarding schools normally only recruit children at the age of seven or eight at the earliest, only keep them within the school during term time, and do not have a monopoly over the formation of the child's personality. And yet many of those who have been through the public-school system have suffered a narrowing of the personality, a cramping of the emotions that remain with them for the rest of their lives. The kibbutz has an infinitely more pervasive influence on its members, for it is the only world the children know, and as a result the characteristics, the symptoms that afflict some of those educated at public schools are to be found in the kibbutz products almost inevitably and in a greatly exaggerated form.

To Women's Lib this flatness of emotional life is probably a virtue—interpreted as an absence of "family chauvinism," an absence of strong attachments toward members of a nuclear family that preclude feelings of affection and humanity for those outside the "right little, tight little" family. The concept of nuclear-family chauvinism is, of course, total nonsense, if only because the nuclear family is too small to be a chauvinistic unit; it is too small to encompass all of an individual's loyalties, too small to be the basis of discrimination, dividing the world into the chosen and the rejected. In fact, chauvinism is much more likely to be a characteristic of the larger substitutes for the nuclear family. The kibbutz is an intensely chauvinistic unit, in a way that the nuclear family could never be. The total immersion of the kibbutznik in the kibbutz is almost by definition exclusive of all outsiders, while the nuclear family cannot and does not demand such exclusive immersion and allegiance. The nuclear family is not just less chauvinistic than the kibbutz—it is also much less chauvinistic than the extended family. We have not heard of many *nuclear* families involving themselves in Mafia-type conspiracies and vendettas! The nuclear family is not big enough to form a football team, let alone to pursue a vendetta.

It would be unfair, however, to assess the success or failure of the kibbutz in terms of the intense chauvinism of these tightly knit communities. The kibbutz alternative to the nuclear family has failed, even without reference to this criterion, and this failure expresses itself at different levels. The kibbutz has failed to abolish the nuclear family, which lives on in a restricted way within its walls. Insofar as it has restricted the life of the nuclear family, it has created severe problems for its individual members which, whether recognized or repressed, fundamentally limit their lives and personalities. The kibbutz has failed to involve more than a tiny minority of the Israelis, and the bulk of the population remains unimpressed by the "virtues" of the alternative to the nuclear family that exists in their midst. Family values remain strong: a research team from the Hebrew University, in a survey of Israeli women, found that three quarters of them thought being "a good mother and a good homemaker" was woman's finest role. Only 8 percent of the married women saw having a job outside their home as "a means of self-expression."[59] All attempts to create kibbutzim in urban areas have failed. "Kibbutzim can exist only (it seems) if the group life is not interfered with by meeting non-group members at every step."[60] This severely limits participation of the kibbutz in the Israeli economy and Israeli society; the kibbutz, then, is an archaic institution in a rapidly developing society that demands mobility, exchange and interaction. In fact, if it were not for high-pressure recruitment of adolescents, the kibbutzim would dwindle in numbers. Many people leave their kibbutz every year and the numbers can only be replenished by exploiting the immature idealism of members of Jewish youth movements in Israel and abroad.

The failure of the kibbutz is particularly salient because all the external circumstances were conducive to its success. The kibbutzim were set up in a new country which enabled its members to break geographically, as well as socially, with their origins; the kibbutz movement was part of the intensely ideological and nationalistic Zionist movement, whose fervor was maintained and increased by a perpetual need to battle against external enemies, a need that strengthened the coherence of the institution; the kibbutz was founded by men and women who were reacting against the intensely introverted ghetto family where the walls of prejudice outside bounced any feelings of anger and resentment back into the family like the cushions on a billiard table—a hardly typical nuclear family atmosphere against which to rebel.

"The kibbutz is dead, long live the family!" is not the basis of my argument. The family must be preserved because of what it is and not because of the failure of those alternatives that have been tried and the absurdity of those merely suggested. Even R. D. Laing, in a recent television interview, retracted his harsh attacks on the family and paid a warm tribute to it: "Some of the happiest, and most fulfilling, rewarding, pleasant and memorable experiences have been in families in which I have lived myself."[61] The right to have a family and to make the role of wife and mother the central role in a woman's life is taken as axiomatic by middle-class and prosperous working-class women. In the same way, as the value of motherhood is revealed through the feelings of women unable to have children, the value of family life is most forcefully demonstrated by the feelings of those women who have seen it curtailed by economic or social pressures. This is the fate of the poor in the West and of most women in Eastern Europe. One Russian journalist with a small child expressed the feelings of many women when she wrote: "Why in a socialist state shouldn't we admit that it is socially useful to bring up children? Why should a woman have to go to work to support her family —unless she wants to—and turn her child over to a stranger who is paid to do the job the mother would like to do? . . . I'm glad it worked out that I had to stay home the first year. I would have missed a lot of precious experiences with my baby if I had gone back to work right away. That's why I think we have to revise the law that only gives a woman fifty-six days' paid leave. It's not enough."[62]

If Women's Lib is to be believed, this Russian journalist should never have felt these dissatisfactions, let alone dared to express them. Her feelings would be branded as either nonexistent or inauthentic. Built into the Women's Lib model are assumptions which make it impossible for it to be adapted to the express desires of women. A British housewife, in a letter to *The Sunday Times,* complained that "indoctrinated as we now are by Women's Lib, none of us doubts the value of a job . . . What we are *not* allowed to believe in is the value of time spent in the family. Why should it be considered more important or more satisfying to give one's skills outside the family rather than in it?"[63]

But such views and desires cannot be accommodated by Women's Lib, and are therefore swept aside. This contradiction between the Women's Lib model of what women's wishes are, and the actual desires of women, is not their only departure from reality. The other major contradiction is between the Women's Lib portrayal of what women are like in their roles as mothers and wives and the actuality of women's behavior.

The image of the limited housewife imprisoned in a closed-off cloister and forced to "stoop" all day long to the intellectual level of her infants remains all-pervasive, despite strong factual evidence about women's increasing experimentation with a variety of roles and life patterns. Women's Libbers have a way of taking a pseudophotographic model of reality and investing it with feelings, fears and frustrations that have a lot to do with caricatures and prototypes but very little to do with real people. It is about time we disentangled the description of the routine work of the "universal housewife" from the emotions of despair that are assumed to be inextricably tied up with housewifery.

The myth of the homogeneous, universal housewife is successfully exploded by Helena Znaniecki Lopata's findings about the great variation in the orientation and involvement of the American wife and mother: "Women in the same stage of the life cycle vary not only in the role upon which they focus (husband, home, child, or career-orientated) but in the manner in which they perceive their obligations."[64] At the one extreme is the woman who handles her world with no initiative and with an entirely uncreative approach to the problems she has to solve, concentrating exclusively on the task aspects of marriage. She is the woman who carries out her role not only minimally and passively but almost apologetically. At the other extreme is the woman who performs her role as housewife, wife and mother in a complex, involved way with interest and originality, drawing from a variety of sources of knowledge and skill. The cluster of the roles of housewife is intrinsically indeterminate; no clear criteria can be applied to how successfully it is carried out, and few roles are as dependent on the self-motivation of the individual if their potential for involvement and fulfillment in a great number of facets of life is to be realized.

Lopata divides housewives into three distinct categories based on the data she has collected: the "restricted," the "uncrystallized" and the "multi-dimensional" housewife.[65] The restricted housewife is effectively the Women's Lib stereotype of all housewives; she is only one type of housewife but has been bandied around as the sole and universal type. The uncrystallized housewife lacks self-confidence and sufficient motivation to take an active part in the wider community, but is anxious to arrange and organize her life rather than to simply let things happen and passively adjust to them. The multi-dimensional housewife is the most interesting, the least mentioned—and never conceded by

Women's Lib—yet the fastest-growing group. She is the housewife of the future—and still a housewife:

> The third type of housewife expresses attitudes which may represent a new personality trend . . . Increased education, income and freedom of life styles are facilitating an expansion of role conceptualizations beyond the prior restrictions. The modern housewife is very likely to define homemaking as extending into the community, mothering as utilizing all societal facilities to expand the world of the young, and wifehood as many-levelled involvement in the various social roles of the husband. In spite of the complexity she assigns to these roles, the same woman is the most likely to think of self-expressive and creative roles for herself and to feel obligations to the society and to the community in which she functions. She gives the impression that the role of housewife provides her with a base for building a many-faceted life, an opportunity few other vocational roles allow, because they are tied down to single organizational structures and goals.[66]

The intransigent insistence of Women's Lib on completely paranoid claims can only retard the achievement of greater opportunities for the category of women who are equally strongly committed to a happy family and a successful career. Sally Oppenheim, a British Member of Parliament, made this point clearly in the debate on the reintroduction of the Anti-Discrimination Bill: "Their extreme views and arguments, their tendency to emphasize the trivial and trivialize what is serious, combine to create hostility rather than support for this Bill."

At the moment the accommodation of part-time or interrupted careers, far from being an integral part of the structure of organizations committed to the employment of women, is regarded as a privilege to be granted only in a haphazard fashion and as a concession rather than a right. There is an urgent need to provide women with a range of employment opportunities and flexible career patterns, "breeding" months or even years, and retraining programs so that the woman who wants to combine successfully her involvement in her career with her family can do so with the minimum of strain. The strength and validity of these demands can only be eroded by their association with the extreme and unpalatable claims of Women's Liberation.

This "multi-dimensional" woman may need assisting; she does not need liberating. This view of the married woman's world may need encouragement if it is to spread; it will certainly not receive it from those who wish to abolish the "occupation housewife" altogether. In fact, by spreading anxiety among women about their roles as women, wives, mothers, Women's Lib will greatly hinder the move toward the female woman of the future; some women will petrify where they are, while others will chase the mirage of liberation in a bewildered fashion.

The Working Woman

... sex role assigns domestic service and attendance upon
infants to the female, the rest of human achievement, interest, and ambition to the male. The limited role allotted the
female tends to arrest her at the level of biological experience. Therefore, nearly all that can be described as distinctively human rather than animal activity (in their own way
animals also give birth and care for their young) is largely
reserved for the male.

—KATE MILLETT[1]

Thus spake the superwoman, high priestess of Women's Lib.

But what do most men know of "human achievement, interest
and ambition"? It sounds very fine but what can men working on
car assembly lines or adding up rows of figures in the dingy
offices of the Internal Revenue or performing other trivial tasks
all day long understand by it? Any one of these is less rewarding
than the role of mother. Women can experience their own kind
of creativity in the family, but very few men have jobs epitomizing
"human achievement, interest and ambition." Kate Millett has
been a sculptor in the morning, taught literature in the after-
noon, invented philosophies in the evening. Perhaps such experi-

83

ences are so gratifying that to be torn away from them by the need to take care of children is frustrating. But most men are not so fortunate—most jobs are imprisoning, not creative. A man with creative aspirations trapped in such a job because he has a family to support is even less able to express his ambitions than a woman with children. She can organize her life to leave some time for developing her own personal interests. A man cannot— his work is organized for him and when he retires, it may well be too late.

Kate Millett calls motherhood "animal," and by implication, finds it degrading. Yet most of our activities can be derived from the animal in this way. The man who works in a factory to earn money to feed his family is comparable with his "animal" ancestors who hunted the woolly rhinoceros. But they are not identical, nor is human motherhood the same as that of animals. A human child is dependent on the mother for a far longer period and requires a far more complex upbringing than does a young animal. There is a qualitative difference between human and animal motherhood as great as between human and animal food-gathering. To see human motherhood as merely animal, as not distinctly human, is simply inverted anthropomorphism.

The Women's Libbers' view of the rival attractions of work and motherhood is an extremely lopsided one. The answer lies in their atypical experience of the world of work as artists (Kate Millett), writers or academics (Germaine Greer, Eva Figes, Shulamith Firestone). They assume that the specific kind of creative activity that is the core of their chosen calling is, or ought to be, the key human pursuit. Everyone ought to be striving for the same kind of satisfaction—a satisfaction only to be attained through work—that they themselves enjoy. The tasks that men and women perform either at work or at home are judged by whether they provide an opportunity for the narrowly defined "creativity" of the intellectual. They ignore the fact that there are other forms of creativity and that there are many "noncreative" ways in which people can obtain enjoyment and fulfillment from their work. They treat fulfillment and frustration as entirely autonomous, entirely independent of the current values of society, and completely ignore that fulfillment in life is, in fact, for most people socially determined. It does not necessarily lie in artistic or intellectual achievement. A lot of people feel happy, feel fulfilled in their tasks, because they have "done their duty"— because they have been good lawyers or bricklayers, typists or housewives. It ill becomes the intellectual to sneer at these people and to dismiss their aspirations as "false" needs. They perform tasks that are vital to society and they derive pleasure from this. If they should choose to cease being producers and consumers or, come to think of it, men and women (for this too impels them to work, to serve, to consume), the intellectual would starve. There is little creative challenge in the work of a chiropodist, but the man with ingrown toenails is rarely disposed to be critical.

Women's Lib, like many other trendy, progressive movements, has made a fetish of creativity in the restricted sense of original artistic or scientific achievement. For them, what is important about creativity is not the results but the experience. In kindergarten the child who is "discovering" the meaning of volume by tipping water from one vessel to another is supposed to emit squeaks of delight at his discovery. The fact that he may simply enjoy pointlessly sloshing water around is either ignored, denied or considered irrelevant. Yet the fallacy ultimately does rest on results. It is tacitly assumed that the creators of works of genius must be happy, that creativity is extremely satisfying and that therefore everyone should strive to be creative. In fact, there is no evidence that creative people are specially happy; for some artists, satisfaction resides in the success of their efforts, not in the efforts themselves, which may indeed be agonizing. Tolstoy hated the process of writing *Anna Karenina*.[2] Would it have been worth it if he had written like Edgar Rice Burroughs? Is there any point in creative effort without talent, in being a fad poet or an incompetent painter? Could a man be said to have a vocation to be a second-rate potter?[3]

The progressive illusion that there is something intrinsically satisfying about low-level creativity is a dangerous one. Everyone is urged to be creative and the alternative incentives of duty or less demanding pleasures are devalued. For the grievance-mongers and the anxiety-makers, to be a good mother is inferior to being a bad sculptor. This would lead to an anomic situation where everyone is filled with a longing for this mysterious creative satisfaction—ever elusive and will-o'-the-wisp. "Creative work," however undisciplined, is expected to lead to instant bliss. Writing is replaced by improvisation, painting by action daubing, music by spontaneous noise! Watch out, here comes instant mathematics accompanied by authentic chemistry. Where standards of achievement are not stressed, where skills are not fostered, such creativity is pointless, boring, disillusioning, and its disciples drop out as fast as they dropped in. Yet, curiously, the fiction is kept up that such activities are a form of work, for the ideology demands that only work is creative. Hence the Libbers' rapture at the oddly named "poetry workshops," "arts laboratories," "experimental theaters" with their connotations of disciplined endeavor that ill describes the undirected, disorganized activities of many of these pseudocreatives.

Women are prominent in these organizations, just as they dominate the older, squarer community evening classes on creative writing or *ikebana,* pottery or recorder playing—they are not excluded from the exciting world of the "creative." Indeed they never were, even when they were excluded from most other occupations. In the past, when women were prevented from being doctors or lawyers, politicians or stockbrokers, they were nevertheless at the forefront of novel-writing and acting, ballet and singing.

If creative achievement is recognized as only one source of

satisfaction in one's work, woman's two roles at home and at work can be compared with man's work-dominated life more realistically and less hysterically. The fundamental assumption of Women's Lib is that at work, men's careers must be much more fulfilling than women's because they are able to commit themselves fully to their job, to acquire more skills and to go on ascending the career ladder faster and further.

Is the life of the top business executive who works sixty hours a week making money less limited than his wife's, who can bring up her children, have a part-time job if she wishes, and depending on her personality, her interests and her imagination, lead an existence more varied than anything he dreams of, if he is still capable of having dreams at all: "For me time is more valuable than money. Time to look after my home properly, time for my husband and children, time for painting and reading, time to study at evening classes, time for voluntary work, time for all the things which make life worthwhile for me."[4]

Even among less affluent groups, a woman may find her work less irksome than her husband does because she does not see it as her central role. Even if her work is boring, it often does not involve her to the same extent; it does not make her feel diminished as a person because she is not defined by herself or by other people in terms of her job. A man, by contrast, is his job. A man's status is judged by his occupational success. A woman's status depends also on her success as wife and mother, and on her husband's occupation as well as her own. Women are in this way curiously more equal than men. Only a few men are a "success" at their job, but most women are competent wives and mothers. For this reason, men experience unemployment as demeaning in a way that women do not. This is true even when the man is unemployed through no fault of his own. Georges Simenon describes well the feelings of a man who could not work because his hands had been blown off in the war and whose wife was out at work all day supporting them:

87

In the first place did people realize he was not leading a man's life? There again in their household the roles were reversed. It was his wife who went away to work in the morning, came back at lunchtime all steeped in the life outside, left again afterwards and didn't get home till evening. And what about him meanwhile? He stayed at home like most wives; waited, cooked the stewed liver—he must take care not to let it burn. He could while away the time by saying to himself, after a glance at the clock, Nelly's doing this . . . Nelly's doing that . . . But what did he really know about it? Wives who stayed at home all day must sometimes feel the same doubts about their husbands.[5]

Perhaps it is not such a man's world, after all. A man who fails to work is scorned or pitied. He is not "leading a man's life." If the Women's Libbers have their way, all will be subject equally to the tyranny of work. The woman who stays at home, even for a good reason, will feel all the doubts and inadequacies of the unemployed man.

Even in the professions, a man will probably have a career in which he has little choice about what he does or how he does it. It is very difficult for a man to refuse promotion, even if it means a move from an interesting or relaxed post to a tedious and stressful one. There are immense pressures on a man to fight his way to the top, even though he may find nothing when he gets there. The lecturer quits his research for the banal administrative duties of professorship, the teacher quits the stimulus of the classroom for the responsibilities of a headship, the doctor is impelled toward a consultant post. There must be no quitting, no turning aside from the rat race to an oasis of quiet or interest or fulfillment. Get on or get out, as Mr. Polly found,[6] and the only "out" for most men is an ulcer or a coronary. A woman, however, can opt out in a way not permitted to men. This possibility is well described in a recent report entitled *Women in Top Jobs:*

Women are more likely than men to have what might be called a general rather than a specialized (or a horizontal rather than a vertical) type of ambition; to be interested in balancing family or leisure interests against work and to settle for a satisfying job which leaves room for this, rather than to drive towards the peak of a profession . . .[7]

A good example of women's freedom from the pressures of ambition and status is the recent decline of the headmistress. Girls' schools regularly advertise for a headmistress saying "Women only need apply," i.e., there is deliberate discrimination in favor of women. But very few women apply and those who do may well fail to meet the requirements of the job. The appointing committee is then forced to readvertise, omitting the discriminatory phrase, and like as not a man is appointed "headmistress." Even in a situation that favors them, women may well prefer to stay in a job which they enjoy and which is not too demanding rather than to take the "liberated" step of getting in there and fighting it out for power and status.

A similar analysis can be made of women in white-collar jobs. Secretarial work may at times be boring and frustrating, but it is not more so than the equivalent male jobs in lower and middle management which also carry much more stress and strain. The main advantage the women have over the men is, once again, freedom. Female secretaries are able to work as temporaries and experience a variety and independence in their work largely denied to men. They are not trapped by a career ladder to which they must hang on like grim death, struggling from rung to rung, hoping against hope to succeed "old Boggins" as deputy assistant acting temporary manager, and dreading the day when a rung snaps and plunges the climber into the proletarian abyss. This freedom to change about is true of women in all jobs, as figures of labor turnover show.[8] Also, women typically work less overtime (average hours worked—men forty-six hours, women thirty-eight hours). Of course these differentials are often the result of the restriction of overtime available to women, but it is also true that many women can afford to take a more relaxed attitude to working hours and are more likely to take odd days off if they don't feel like going in or if there are problems over the children. Naturally, where there is a high rate of absenteeism in any case (and this is increasingly true of repetitive manual jobs in high-wage economies), male workers may also take time off for more personal pursuits—usually infinitely more frivolous. This is certainly a feature of much of the latest statistical evidence in America and is clearly seen in the figures for absenteeism in the wholly male preserve of coal mining in the United Kingdom.

Female manual workers are usually forced to take tedious unskilled jobs, but these at least are not as exhausting as unskilled jobs performed by men. Where there *is* serious discrimination is that women are excluded from skilled craftsmen's jobs. Women's assembly jobs require very little attention, so that they can talk or listen to the radio while they work. They need not be involved with their work in any sense.

The woman is outside her task, the man is eaten up by his. Men often take jobs which totally occupy them but do not fulfill them. They take such jobs because they are highly paid, but then they are trapped in them, like a wasp in a jam jar, by their family's ongoing financial commitments—mortgage, installment buying, repairs on the car. Effectively the man sacrifices the central meaning of his life (as defined by society)—his work—so that his wife can attain the central purpose of hers—a good home for the family.

Women, then, tend to be protected from the worst tasks. The main areas from which they are totally or largely excluded are tough, dangerous and disagreeable—mining, dock working, combat roles in the armed forces, the merchant marine, the fire service. Even in mixed areas, such as the police, the men complain that they are landed with more than their fair share of the most unpleasant jobs—night work, shift work, heavy work, dangerous work. Man's lot in the world of work is not better than woman's over the whole spectrum. It is simply more varied; there is simply a greater divergence from the average. Men are more likely to be found in the worst jobs as well as the best ones.[9]

It is, in fact, artificial to separate job satisfaction from sexual role playing at all. In very few of the things we do are our pleasures and discontents intrinsic to the task itself. Rather, we derive pleasure from fulfilling a purpose society has instilled in us. There are no "true needs" and "false needs," though perhaps biological factors predispose us to seek some gratifications more than others. Biology and social conditioning, then, the innate and the experienced, go hand in hand, as in the case of the male and female roles that people play. Men in jobs that are, on the face of it, boring or dangerous often find them satisfying because "it's a man's job" to be a miner or a truckdriver, to operate a huge press for making castings, or to fly a bomber. This means that men are motivated to perform these unpleasant, yet vital tasks; if it also means that the men involved in these tasks feel satisfied, then sexual role playing of this kind can be justified on utilitarian grounds. There is no reason why such pleasures should be less valued than those derived by a mediocre craftsman from his "creative" work. Creativity is only meaningful where there is talent, and to make it the only or central satisfaction that is to be derived from work is to arrogantly rub most people's noses in their own mediocrity. The untalented have a right to recognition, too, and the expression of their manhood or womanhood through their work is one way of achieving this.

For women, of course, the chief mode of expressing themselves through work is in the family. Being a wife and mother is an occupation just as certainly as being a bus driver or a businessman. The bread-maker is as important as the breadwinner and has just as certainly a *real* job. The problem is not that housewives do not have an occupation, but that our conventional definition of an occupation is inadequate. A housewife has an occupation, yet the language we use to describe people's jobs fails to recognize it. One American has sought to overcome the poverty of our definitions by calling the housewife a homemaker and her work domestic engineering. The card-catalogue description of Mary Stranahan Pattison's book *The Business of Home Management* in the

Library of Congress epitomizes this attempt to make the housewife's tasks more prestigious by linguistic gymnastics: "The principles of domestic engineering; an attempt to evolve a solution to the domestic 'labor and capital' problems—to standardize and professionalize housework—to reorganize the house upon 'scientific management' principles and to point out the importance of the public and personal element therein, as well as the practical."[10]

This sounds pretentious and artificial because we continue in our hearts to define "real" work as involving a contract, a pay check, and a social security card. Only when we have the sense to drop this assumption will we be able to transcend the conventional terminology. The attempt by Women's Libbers to make the relationship of a woman to her family a contractual one with a pay check and, no doubt, social security, pension and workmen's compensation, with one month's notice on either side and a gold watch after twenty-five years' loyal service, is as silly an attempt to ape the male world as that of the home engineers.[11] The need is to recognize woman's role at home as important in its own right and not simply because it can be matched with male occupations or expressed in pseudoscientific terminology.

How satisfying is the "occupation housewife" when compared with other jobs? The valid comparison is, of course, with the kind of job the average man does—the laborer, the office clerk, the factory worker, the plumber—and not with those rare, exciting and stimulating jobs that the Women's Libbers assume to be the norm. Whatever criterion we now apply—results, freedom, variety, creativity, interest, personal contact—the average housewife comes off better than her average husband.

Germaine Greer fails to see this: "A housewife's work has no results: it simply has to be done again. Bringing up children is not a real occupation, because children come up just the same, brought or not."[12] What results does a "real occupation" have? What job does not have to be done again? Does the man who makes a tenth part of a fender nine hundred times a day enjoy, or even see, the results of his work? The lawyer who has done the titling on ten thousand houses, the accountant who has filed innumerable tax returns, the academic stumbling through last year's lecture notes, the miner hacking his way along an endless seam of coal—do they see a tangible result of their labor?

Do children "come up just the same"? Did little Germaine Greer come up just the same? "Once my mother knelt on my small brother's chest and beat his face with her fists . . . after nagging and badgering her eldest child into running away from home (a fact which she concealed for years by talking of her as if she were present, when she knew absolutely nothing of what she was doing) . . ."[13] Did the monkey with the cloth mother come up just the same?[14]

Does a cared-for child come up just the same as a neglected or persecuted one?[15] Does any mother believe that her child would grow up happy and capable without her care and love? Happy children do not "come up" just the same, though unhappy ones probably do. Germaine Greer's fatalistic view of the child's development is about as accurate as the medieval belief that disease was inevitable and brought about by God. People died off "just the same." In the past this view relieved parents of the responsibility for the physical health of their children in the same way that Germaine Greer's view implies that parents can do nothing to influence the personality, temperament and intelligence of their children. To have a child at all is a creative act and one which no man can experience. Indeed, some men positively resent and envy this female privilege. Man's role in conception is soon over; it is the woman who creates the baby. Language here is on the side of women, for men are often forced to describe their creative activities in terms that belong to women. The man "gives birth" to a theory, the woman to a child.

Our current obsession with creativity is the result of our continued striving for immortality in an era when most people no longer believe in an afterlife.[16] Now we must create our own heaven and hell on earth. For a few, it is their creative work in the arts or the sciences, their ability to somehow transform the world; for the many, immortality means children, descendants, family. They wish to care for their own genetic descendants— their own creation. Creation has become our chief hope to counter mortality. Motherhood goes on being creative after the child is born, and it is fair to compare her role at its best with that of those rare creative individuals in other occupations, for each mother is unique. What makes a gifted creative person different is that he cannot easily be replaced. The fruits of a woman's work as an artist, a researcher or an entrepreneur are unique, but most women are easily replaced in their jobs by other similarly qualified women. As long as the job is done, it doesn't much matter who does it. Society need simply insist that the person be competent. You cannot replace a George Eliot or a Marie Curie, but you can replace accountants, lawyers, schoolteachers, typists, factory workers. To the plant manager, operatives are as standardized and replaceable as pieces of machinery. All that matters about them is what they do in aggregate. Have we got enough of them? Are they, in general, competent? The fate of any one individual is almost irrelevant.

You may be able to swap typists easily, but you cannot swap mothers. One mother is not as good as another. Because the mother works in a small group based on intimate personal relationships, she is irreplaceable, she is a uniquely valuable individual, valuable as well as unique; this must be stressed, for even those who admit a mother's unique function often treat motherhood as a poor substitute for "really" creative work, a sublimation. Simone de Beauvoir mocks those who believe that motherhood "is a greater work than penetrating the futile secrets of the atom."[17] (O that the secrets of the atom had been futile!) But how many men probe the atom every day? How much of what men do is as important as creating a happy childhood and a fully developed human being? Nor is this an easy accomplishment. Helena Znaniecki Lopata, who has systematically studied the lives of American housewives in a way that no Women's Libber has ever attempted, concluded: "The responsibility heaped upon a mother of meeting the almost contradictory goals of bringing up her children into both adjustment and creativity, popularity and achievement, excellence in a speciality and multi-dimensional ability could possibly be carried out by a highly trained psychologist lacking any personality problems dysfunctional to the attempt."[18] Perhaps this is not as vivid as the rantings of Women's Lib, but it is based on more substantive findings than an ill-remembered unhappy childhood, or a well-remembered miserable marriage, hysterically projected onto all other marriages and childhoods.

The housewife, far from being a captive of her work, has far more freedom in it than most men. She does not have to work at the speed of the conveyor belt or the dictates of the foreman. She is free from the discipline of stopwatch and dial, clocking in and clocking out, rule book and bureaucrat. Her world is large enough to be challenging, small enough to be meaningful. She can choose to farm out to a specialized agency those aspects of her work which are more arduous and rely increasingly on factory pre-preparations. The laundromat and the can opener are within every housewife's reach. In the future, the automatic dishwasher or even the out-of-work actor lugging expensive spring-cleaning equipment from door to door will be as widely available. She will be free to concentrate on the one task that cannot be standardized—personal relations.

The need of both sexes to be involved in a meaningful activity and see an end result to their work is well expressed in the booming do-it-yourself interest. Even those men who lack any interest in their everyday work fling themselves eagerly into papering the walls, painting the ceilings, demolishing weeds in the garden. In these home activities, the husband shows an enthusiasm and a dedication that his boss never sees. Like his wife he is working for himself and his family, like her he sees an end product to his work, like her he works in his own time and at his own pace.

This is not a plea for Men's Lib. Whether or not a man chooses to accept the social pressures associated with the male stereotype is an individual decision. There are no legal or institutional barriers that prevent a man from exercising his right to live off his wife's moral earnings. There is no cause to be fought. The position of women is different. There still remain legal and institutional barriers that prevent women from freely entering certain occupations. Women's emancipation demands that these barriers should be done away with, immediately. They restrict women's range of choice and they provide a genuine grievance that adds respectability to the fundamentally different and unacceptable demands of Women's Liberation.

There is probably some case to be made for protecting women from certain kinds of physical strain or danger. It would be foolish, for example, to allow women to lift as heavy loads as men. However, most restrictions are entirely outmoded. Many jobs that once required male strength are now easily managed by a woman. Many jobs in the docks are now done by fork-lift trucks or container cranes, and there will be very little physical toting around of heavy goods in the future. With power steering, most heavy-goods vehicles are as easy to drive as a Ford. The rules in those industries which exclude women are archaic survivals of a day when these jobs were much tougher than they are now, in terms of both muscular effort and danger. It is equally difficult to see why the Department of Employment should need to grant a special dispensation to allow women to work night shifts (only six thousand do so in England at any one time) or to work more than forty-eight hours a week.[19] Women who are doctors or nurses regularly work long hours through the night. Why should they not be allowed to do so in industry?

The main discrimination against women in industry comes from the trade unions, who systematically exclude women from skilled manual jobs. Only union restrictions prevent women bus drivers in London—no real physical bar can be upheld. The unions always pay lip service to women's rights, but not when it comes to apprenticeships. They are a big stumbling block, obstructing the legitimate occupational demands of women to be bus drivers, carpenters or electricians. It is easier for a woman to get a Ph.D. than to drive a steam shovel.

However, even if the restrictions imposed on women by the government or the unions are abolished, it is exceedingly unlikely that a state of affairs would arise where men and women do the same jobs. Similarly, even if the legitimate demand for equal pay is enforced, it is unlikely to result in men and women having the same aggregate earnings. Germaine Greer, in fact, expressed skepticism about the value of equal-pay legislation on just these grounds:

> Perhaps women should be glad that Mr William Hamilton's Private Member's Bill to render illegal discrimination by employers on the grounds of sex was talked out in the Commons . . . If Mr Hamilton's Bill had demanded that all employers show an *equal* distribution of men and women in all parts of their enterprise it might have forcibly wrenched asunder the vicious circle of women's position in the work force . . .[20]

The aim of the Anti-Discrimination Bill is clearly emancipation. Germaine Greer's goal is liberation, though she did admit that "it would also have wrecked what remains of the British economy."[21] Among the reasons why it would wreck the British economy which are not mentioned by Germaine Greer are the marked differences in innate capacity for different kinds of work of men and women.

One survey summed up the differences in physical strength: "Adult women have only 65 per cent of the strength of adult men. Part of this is due to the fact that they are smaller but even allowing for this, their strength is still markedly lower than men. Most industrial activities involve the use of the arms and arm strength is the area of greatest difference between men and women. The overall working capacity of women is on average about 30 per cent lower than that of men. In a study comparing

97

work output between men and women in the same task Dunstch, Stoboy and Mellorwirzch (1962) found at the end of the work period that the work output was: for men 12,700 mkg per 10 minutes, for women 7,500 mkg per 10 minutes. In this particular study women achieved 68 per cent of the work efficiency of men."[22]

In addition, in tasks involving movement, men have faster reaction times than women. This is true for movements of feet, hands and arms.[23] Women by contrast are superior in manual dexterity and accuracy. They are more likely to be skillful and deft with their hands and hence make better seamstresses, needlewomen, typists and assemblers of small components.[24]

H. Fairweather and S.J. Hutt sum up the differences in skill and reaction time between men and women: ". . . tasks upon which females are superior seem to be based mainly upon past experience and extensive prior practice; they involve relatively little mediation by higher cortical processes; they contain little or no response to novelty; they characteristically involve fine co-ordination of small muscles and place a premium upon speed and accuracy of response rather than upon the production of new responses or insights. The paradigm case is that of typing. The tasks upon which males are superior generally involve inhibition or delay of response to obvious stimulus attributes; they involve mediation by higher cortical processes and are evaluated in terms of finding a solution to a problem as opposed to speed and accuracy of response."[25]

It isn't, then, entirely accidental or deliberately discriminating that most typists or telephone operators are women, most skilled workers men. When we add to this Dr. Corinne Hutt's finding that "women are able to hold in their memory store for short periods of time a number of unrelated and personally irrelevant facts, whereas men are only capable of comparable memory feats if the material is personally relevant or coherent,"[26] we can see why most routine clerical work is assigned to women.

The finding that men and women differ in mental abilities is more controversial than statements of differences in size or strength. The latter is too obvious to be denied, but a belief in differences in ability can still be denounced as sexist. Yet, as shown elsewhere, these do exist and are a result of the profound, innate distinctions between men and women. They are summed up in the table below.

The contents of the table can be summarized by saying that women excel in verbal and men in nonverbal abilities. Men are superior in the logical manipulation of concepts and relationships whether these involve numbers, words, patterns or spatial relations; women are superior in verbal fluency and execution.[27] On the *average* there is no difference in the overall intelligence of the sexes—they simply possess different kinds of ability and excel in different ways. Men's abilities and interests equip them for dealing with objects and abstractions, women's for dealing with people.[28] Men can put a man on the moon but how well can they handle the relational problems on earth?

Men's abilities are better geared than women's to running an industrial society based primarily on manufacturing, but the

ABILITIES AND APTITUDES

WOMEN SUPERIOR	MEN SUPERIOR
Verbal fluency. Verbal "execution" (reading, writing, spelling, enunciation, sentence construction).	Verbal reasoning, comprehension, analytical thinking. Ability to abstract something without being distracted by its context.
Discrimination and/or comparison of fine visual detail, visual matching, visual search.	Numerical tasks. Visual tasks involving spatial relationships. Spatial perception and organization. Mechanical aptitude and reasoning.
Rote memory.	Problem solving involving the breaking of a mental set.

99

fastest-growing sector in that society is services—both public and private—and it is here that women come into their own. The male-oriented, mechanical interpretation of women's equality put forward by Women's Lib stems from an already obsolescent view of the industrial economy. A manufacturing economy places a premium on such qualities as aggression, persistence and concentration. By contrast, in a service society the key occupational skill required is the ability to relate to other people and to interact with them person to person. Here such female qualities as cooperation, nurturance and an ability to do several jobs at once are more important. The previously mentioned report *Women in Top Jobs* emphasizes the need for the specifically female qualities, not just in services but also in humanizing all large companies:

> Even more important than commodities, moreover, will be the increasing scope for the specialist, particularly in services which could be independent or under the umbrella of the parent organization. Most important of all, while the criteria governing the size of large companies are partly technical and economic partly acquisitive and defensive in nature, the remoteness of authority, the depersonalization of work, the routine and monotony of jobs, serve to underline the overriding importance of communications, an aspect of business life to which the women we interviewed attach the greatest importance and which they profitably exploit.[29]

It is vitally important to stress that all statistics about the differences in abilities between men and women as groups are irrelevant to the issue of equal opportunities for men and women as individuals. On balance, men may have higher nonverbal and lower verbal ability than women but this will not necessarily be true for any one pair of individuals. If selection is free of sex bias and based on merit only, the result will still be that men will be preponderant in certain occupations but the minority of women who are as well fitted to such posts will be able to compete on equal terms.

Because men and women have different kinds of abilities, it is clear that they are suited to different—not inferior or superior—tasks. In today's society some jobs are done by men because they are better suited to them, others because women are unfairly excluded. This is a distinction Women's Lib fails to draw. If women were fully emancipated, and the day of "liberation" had not come upon us, there would not be a marked change in the sex composition of all jobs but some areas where men now predominate would be taken over by women. Equality of opportunity would result in only a small rise in the numbers of women accountants, engineers or geologists but a big rise in the numbers of female physicians, psychiatrists, lawyers, clergymen. Indeed, women might come to preponderate in these fields. If opportunities were really equal—as they should undoubtedly be—there would be a fairer representation of women in the various professions and occupations, but their distribution between different groups would still be highly skewed. The advantage of such a change would be that women would end up in jobs for which they are suited by ability and temperament, but the Women's Lib goal of equal representation in all sectors and professions would not be attained, even if equal opportunities were established. Where such equality has been established in the kibbutz, there is still a marked disparity in the kinds of jobs men and women do. The response to this of the American Women's Libbers has been to urge that the kibbutz should "draft women to its managerial jobs even if they are not inclined to accept them"![30] Equality of the sexes at work, in the sense of equal representation implied by Women's Lib, has not been achieved in the kibbutz despite the fact that this was a central tenet of the system. The second generation of kibbutz women, secure in the importance of the roles they prefer and confident in their own abilities, do not feel that they have to make a show of their emancipation by shrugging off service occupations and child rearing. They regard their mothers' obsessional fear that they may be restricted to "women's work" and kept from what is really "important" as irrelevant and anachronistic.

The proportion of women in any profession should correspond to the degree to which they choose it and are suited to it. A society which prevents this by discriminating against women and Women's Lib, which demands an arbitrary parity, is equally destructive of women's freedom. One favorite statistic that Women's Lib is fond of quoting is that one third of all engineers in Russia are women, whereas in Britain they comprise less than 1 percent of the total. The British figure may be ludicrously low but, equally, the Russian figure is artifically inflated. Many of these women would have preferred another kind of higher education, but engineering is often the only one open to them.[31]

The reason women go into engineering in large numbers in Eastern Europe is mainly the lack of alternatives; the economies of these countries are geared to heavy industry and armaments, and deliberately neglect consumer goods and services which provide the kind of jobs women *on the average* prefer and are better at. It is also true that engineering is relatively free from political pressures, and many women and men who would pursue arts or social science courses in Western Europe are reluctant engineers in Russia. The crucial questions, then, about the women engineers of Russia are: "Do they enjoy it? Would they prefer to do something else if they had the chance?" In any case, even under Russian conditions, where there is great pressure on women to go into engineering, the men outnumber the women 2 to 1.

The Women's Liberation movement is essentially an upper-middle-class movement which tries to extend its appeal by using the problems of the poorest women in the community as a justification for its radicalism. The support they receive from the poor, however small, only serves to conceal the very real differences in needs and outlook of these various groups of women. We can represent the opportunities and life chances of women in roughly three groups:

A. *Top professionals*   Reluctant to interrupt careers even though they have small children. The "dual-career" family.

B. *"Middle-class norm"*   Women leave labor force temporarily when children are small.

C. *Poor*   Women forced to remain in labor force, though they have small children. The "dual-worker" family.

Each has its own distinctive problems. Despite the attacks of Women's Lib on the bourgeois housewife (which, though called middle class, includes women who are the wives of well-paid manual workers), the average woman finds most fulfillment in belonging to group B—the closest to the norm of society. The economic loss of production and the psychological loss (if any) to the woman leaving her job are small in comparison with the gains in the personal happiness of mother and children. Kate Millett, of course, regards this as an inefficient solution. She writes of the nuclear family as "a wasteful and inefficient body" which works in an "unsystematic and individualistic manner" and which generally precludes "woman's contribution to the larger society."[32] This attitude is surely perverse—the family should be praised, not condemned for not being dominated by the need for bureaucratic efficiency. If only all jobs could be "unsystematic and individualistic"! Who wants the personal relationships so basic to marriage and child care to be characterized by efficiency, systematic planning and uniformity? We might be richer if all women were in the labor force and all children in the care of a small number of professional child-minders, but would we be happier? As we get richer, so the allure of yet more wealth ought to become smaller. Our ideal should be a society where all women can, *if they wish,* afford to leave the labor force while their children are small. Those women who are now in the "poor" category should be assisted by improved welfare arrangements to be able to quit working for a time just like their wealthier counterparts.

The problem of the top professionals in group A is in a special category. These women (few in number but important) are highly talented and do vital, interesting and well-paid jobs. The loss to society and to the women themselves of a prolonged absence from their work is much greater. There is a need for tax concessions that would encourage a greater division of labor by enabling such women to farm out many of their household chores. There is a need for extended maternity leave and for state-run play groups for the under-fives; the greater priority given to the provision of nursery schools is clearly of extreme importance in this context and should be encouraged even further. However, the Women's Lib demand for twenty-four-hour nurseries where children can be dumped indefinitely encourages an abdication of maternal responsibility and should be unnecessary even with group A. Career and maternity are not opposed in this stark way.

In the dual-career family, which would result with group A, there are reciprocal advantages between the fulfillment and involvement in one sphere of life and those originating in another. Women's Lib writers, however, make an unwarranted extension of the reciprocal advantages of the dual-career family to the dual-worker families by treating these two distinct categories as one. Women's Lib dishonestly promises the fulfillment open to group A to all women who take on an outside job. The truth is that for many women the reward of an outside job is not added fulfillment that spills over into the family sphere, but added fatigue that impairs their activities and enjoyment within the family. The goal should be to widen the top group of women, and narrow, if possible to extinction, the bottom group. Even then, it would be dishonest to talk in terms of one homogeneous group of women which benefits largely and identically from the interaction between the family and an outside job.

This emphasis on fulfillment from work as *work,* without reference to its nature, is one of the most anachronistic obsessions of

Women's Lib in an age when the basic working week has been substantially shortened, retirement comes sooner and the boom in leisure demands a shift of emphasis from singing the praises of work as the paramount virtue to viewing leisure as central in our lives and extending our ability and self-motivation to use it imaginatively. "Self-realization in leisure" rather than "self-realization through work" will be the pattern of the future unless we insist on a misplaced asceticism that would make us continue to view institutionalized work as all-important. When widespread affluence comes to the Mediterranean countries, it will be much easier to find converts to the leisure creed; the cult of efficiency and routine so entrenched in the West has been eroded by the Mediterranean sunshine, and the notion that the only worthwhile activities are those that bring in money has never been as widespread.

The Women's Libbers' emphasis on work can only be accepted if you believe, as they obviously do, that rigorous, routine action is admirable, whatever its ultimate goal and even if there is no ultimate goal at all. This enthronement of "action" has meant that knowledge and learning are viewed as important only as ingredients in technical schemes and professional competence. Involvement in voluntary associations is dismissed as killing time, although it is undisputable that, especially in America, without women's voluntary participation many activities would have to be discontinued or converted into recognized occupations or professions. The dethronement of work should bring about a marked change in the location of home in relation to society. A trend that began in the eighteenth century and led to the complete isolation of the home from the mainstream of political and social activities would tend to be reversed, and the home may once again be at the center, or at least much nearer the center, of societal life. The implication for the life of the wife and mother will be dramatic. The stereotype of the uneducated, passive and noninvolved housewife will give way to the image of the female woman who will interact her role of wife, mother and member of the wide community in a complex and creative way, varying according to the different stages of the life cycle. She will be able to bring back to the home the life which has been too rigidly segregated from it for the last two centuries and integrate her political, religious and educational involvement with her home and family life. The obsession with the "masculine," paid job, and the overrated value attached by Women's Lib to nine-to-five work of a clearly defined occupational nature, will appear, even more so than today, extremely irrelevant to women's problems.

This breakup of the barriers between home and work will undoubtedly be regarded by the high priests of "efficiency" as a dilettante and amateurish retrograde step. But as our economy moves from the manufacturing to the service era, the tyranny of routine and efficiency cannot be as persuasively defended, and the "efficient" isolation of home from work will be one of the first bastions to fall.

The Male Man

The Women's Lib ideology is based on two adamantine statements, both of which are wrong. First, it assumes that both men
and women are trapped by sexual stereotypes, and second, that
the stereotyped images to which women must submit are more
oppressive than those men conform to. Women's Libbers do
occasionally admit that male stereotypes cause problems as well,[1]
but this is soon seen as utter hypocrisy: they concede the general
point but quickly brush aside all specific aspects. It is, of course,
necessary to their view of society as "man exploiting and manipulating woman" to demonstrate that men have appropriated for
themselves the good life, the good conditions and the "good
stereotype," leaving women with a hard life, unpleasant conditions and a negative stereotype.

The Women's Libbers are only able to do this because they are
so obsessed with the "wrongs" of women that they never really
come to terms with the question of what life is like for men. As
a result they make many naïve assumptions about the problems
men and women face; there are many difficulties and frustrations
common to both men and women that they treat as distinctively
female problems. Germaine Greer writes of girls in college: "A

girl's emotional welfare is so much a matter of the demeanour of men towards her that she may jeopardize her academic chances by emotional involvement. I can testify to the wasteful effects of emotional involvement on studying women from personal experience as a tutor in universities."[2] And I can testify, from personal experience as a student, that men are equally afflicted; it is absurd to regard emotional involvement and the pain caused by the failure of a relationship as a female preserve. Neither do women have a monopoly of fear, depression, frustration, futility or self-contempt. Yet the reader of the Women's Lib tracts cannot but conclude that these melancholy feelings are reserved for the female sex.

Of course, distinctive problems do exist for women, and these are stridently proclaimed by Women's Lib—so much so that one can almost speak of a women's problems subculture. These have been so exhaustively discussed that a woman who does not share them almost feels abnormal. What is not accepted and certainly not publicized is that the male sex has its own specific problems and that these problems are often more severe than those experienced by women.

Man's distinctive problems start even before he is born. At conception there are 120 males for every 100 females, but among live births there are only 106 males per 100 females and among the male fetuses there are more miscarriages, more male stillbirths.[3] This prenatal vulnerability would be irrelevant to man's distinctive problems but for the fact that this greater vulnerability of the male does not end with birth. Infant mortality is much higher among boys, and male mortality is higher throughout childhood. This difference even extends to emotional disorders. More boys than girls are referred to the child psychiatric services,[4] and there is an even greater preponderance of boys among children suffering from the more severe disorders: boys outnumber girls by 4 to 1 among autistic children.[5]

These facts do not fit into the Women's Lib framework, and so tend to be ignored. By contrast, women's weaknesses and diseases are trumpeted and somehow made part of their social condition. "Nervous diseases, painful menstruation, unwanted pregnancies, accidents of all kinds are all evidence of women's energy destroying them."[6]

How many women were destroyed by menstruation last year? Not many—but many more men than women died early in life of accidents, suicide, heart disease, cancer or respiratory diseases, all diseases that reflect the greater stresses that men undergo. Even respiratory diseases and lung cancer are the result of men trying to combat the strain in their lives by smoking more heavily.[7]

Women's greater longevity, whether due to innate factors or environmental ones, is a harsh fact for Women's Lib. If it is the result of innate differences between the sexes, the Women's Lib thesis that all sex differences are culturally determined collapses; if it is the result of environmental factors, then men are more harshly treated than women and it is their myth of the downtrodden woman that collapses.

Not only is it harder to be a man, it is also harder to become one. The adult the small child knows best is his mother. The small girl learns to be a woman by directly copying her mother and is able to identify with those of her own sex at a much earlier age; she is very early on a little woman. The small boy cannot identify with his father as easily, for he will normally see far more of his mother.[8] In a home where there is no father at all, the boys may well grow up ineffectual and weak. They may become homosexuals or overcompensate by being tough and violent, indulging in assaults, robberies or rape. Even in an ordinary household where the father is a permanent, if evenings-and-the-weekends figure, the small boy will experience greater difficulty in growing up. He has to be enticed and forced to be a man by a mixture of carrots and sticks. The carrot is an artificial portrayal of a man's life as being more adventurous, more exciting, somehow more important and full of glittering prizes. For most boys, the process is successful, and by the age of ten or eleven, boys are convinced

that masculinity is not only their destiny but their preference.
The expressed preference of the boys for masculinity is curiously
similar to the occupational preferences of coal miners. Coal mining is a dirty, dangerous and unpleasant job, much more so than
most other occupations, yet it is difficult to get coal miners to
leave defunct pits to work in light industry. They scornfully reject
such unmasculine work as "doll's-eye factories" that could never
measure up to the grand life of mining—"it's a man's job." The
reason for this bravado, this pride, is that they need to believe it
to go down the pit at all. The harsh facts of danger and unpleas-
antness can only be repressed by a cult of toughness and pride.

Man's role in society is tougher, riskier, often nastier than
woman's. To get men to be men, society needs to give them a
version of the coal miner's pride: small boys are encouraged to
accept a rougher, more dangerous life than their sisters by the
praise and rewards given to "brave little men." Boys behave very
differently from girls for genetic reasons, but if *all* boys are to be
boys, if all boys are to become men, then society must reinforce
these innate dispositions. Primitive cultures clearly acknowl-
edged, by the importance they attached to male initiation rites,
the need to reinforce socially man's inherent tendency toward
masculinity.

Most men do not, of course, become coal miners, sponge div-
ers, locomotive engineers, firemen or bank robbers. They are
more likely to have jobs that do not involve much physical risk
or daring—fitters, electricians, bank managers, lawyers, drafts-
men. But most boys' games, however, do involve some simulated
physical risk and daring. They play cops and robbers, cowboys
and Indians—they dress up as policemen, firemen, soldiers; they
love toy guns, swords, truncheons. They don't play bank managers and cashiers, and there are no miniature three-piece suits for
embryo shyster lawyers, there are no kits for the little assembly-
line operative; stores stock policemen's helmets and ten-gallon
hats for their half-pint customers, but they do not stock bishops'
miters, stockbrokers' homburgs or even trade-unionists' cloth

caps. Even when children are not imitating adults in any simple way, they play games that do not necessarily prepare them for their roles later in life—there is in fact a sharp discontinuity: what relevance do football, rugby or even plain childhood fighting and wrestling have to their later careers?

The boys are being inculcated with a false myth about the adult male world. It is made to look exciting, challenging, risky and adventurous in a direct physical sense, which appeals to them and entices them into masculinity. The myth of masculine glamour is undoubtedly unreal, yet it is symbolically linked to reality. The themes of risk, success, failure, aggression, competition, team-work are common to the world of boys and the world of men. The success or failure of businessmen, artisans, professionals is more subtle versions of childhood winning and losing; victory and defeat. The aggressive cowboy becomes the aggressive salesman; the risks of climbing to the top of a pine tree are replaced by the risks of entrepreneurship. The link between male childhood and adult roles is, however, indirect, subtle and tenuous for most occupations and for most parts of a man's life. The link is strongest and most direct for the man who becomes a soldier. Most countries have some form of conscription, and for most men military service, however short, is an integral part of their lives. Even in Britain, the situation in Ulster has made the army seem much less remote and much less apart from the average man's life.

The transition from the false glamour of masculinity that pervades boys' childhood to the more humdrum adult world is made successfully by most men, but some continue to cling to the glamorous myth: some, like Walter Mitty, drive imaginary tanks when commuting to the office, others seek in delinquency the excitement that was dangled in front of them and then taken away. This is part of the price men have to pay for the positive aspects of masculinity. Perhaps the greatest tribute that the adult man's childhood exacts from him is his eagerness to get into the stands around the edge of a muddy field on a day damp with drizzle, watching twenty-two even muddier men kick a greasy football around—sometimes the ball isn't even round, there are more men and they have to kick the ball over the goal posts instead of between them. Fortunately, only some men pay the tribute at this surtax rate. Many men are able to outgrow the childhood obsession, and one of the more pleasant aspects of England is that more men have been weaned from their footballs than is the case in Greece. My objections to football are not those of the liberated women. They resent it because they are excluded from it; I resent it because I find it irredeemably boring! The stage of liberation no doubt includes the Arsenal team being forced to play against Braless Athletic or Sappho United, and preferably against both at once so that the women can always emerge victorious. In the long run, of course, Women's Lib would expect the female (?) team to win in their own right anyway.

Apart from these minor deviations and a few more serious casualties, men soon abandon the mythology inculcated in them by the *Boy's Life*. Women's Libbers are the sole remaining true believers in the comics' portrayal of the male world as intrinsically superior and more exciting than the female. Millett's view that "human achievement, interest and ambition"[9] are the preserve of men and men alone is, after all, only a sophisticated restatement of the image presented by the comics. It seems to spring from what they thought and felt the masculine world was about when they were ten. At this age, a girl's feminine identity is least secure. Her early identification with her mother has been eroded by contact with the masculinizing effect of the boy's subculture,[10] her adult role is remote and it is much easier to idealize masculine qualities. Germaine Greer shares and exaggerates the feelings of these few tomboy misfits: ". . . [she] may insist on mucking about with boyish affairs, even to the extent of joining a male group and fighting to maintain her place in it by being twice as tough as any of the boys. She may lose all her hankies and hair-ribbons, rip her knickers climbing trees, and swear and swagger with the best of them."[11]

This is the explicit wish of the tomboy, but it is more than that —it is the half-secret dream of the would-be liberated woman, who wants to remake adult life in the image of childhood escapades into masculinity. Ripped knickers become burned bras. This wish to regress into irresponsible childishness is at the heart of all middle-class liberation movements in wealthy societies. The men go back to their own childhood, the women to someone else's. Apart from the ultra tomboy, the tom-tomboy, most women cannot use their own childhood as the basis of their adult fantasy of liberation; unlike the men they have a sex barrier built in to their fantasy, and it is this they wish to remove. Women's Liberation is not so much a protest against currently felt deprivations as a wish to demolish ghostly barriers and phantom memories.

Here we see one more reason for the current upsurge of Women's Liberation movements. In the recent past, when parental influence was the most powerful single factor in a child's upbringing, the sexual identity of the girl, based as it was on direct imitation of her mother, was more secure than that of the boy. Today the impact of peer groups and of cultural factors, such as the mass media, have become an increasing challenge to parental influence. At a time when the boy spends more time with his mother than with his father, these changes may well buttress his masculine identification. But the girl's sexual identity would tend to be weakened and Women's Lib is based on those women whose female identity has now been shaken. The irony is that they attempt to solve the problem of a weak identity by making it even weaker. They claim that the removal of sex differentiation among children is a necessary prelude to attaining full equality for adult women. They want to share the boys' subculture, both the reality and the dreams, though not, perhaps, the nightmares. They want to become "twice as tough as any of the boys"[12] in order to become twice as tough as any of the men, and twice as fast as any male rat in the rat race; when they sorted out the men from the boys, the girls would be men. The Liberationists see this undifferentiated upbringing as the only way to attain parity for women in adult life. The orgy of aggressiveness that would follow can have little appeal for most women or most men. Far from being a necessary evil of the emancipation of women, it would clearly obstruct its achievement. Women have distinctive abilities and qualities; once these have been recognized and given equal value and esteem, the aim should be "more than parity" in jobs where these female qualities are most important rather than parity in all jobs. It would be a sad mistake if women were to use parity of numbers in each occupation as the test of the end of discrimination, and it would be a disaster if they then made futile attempts to achieve this by overhauling girls' upbringing so that only male qualities were valued and inculcated.

There are some masculine roles and attitudes that it is difficult for a woman to adopt—physical aggression in women perhaps provoking the strongest social sanctions—but in general, women have a very wide area of choice and can deviate from the accepted female stereotype as much or as little as they choose. Society is very tolerant of mannish or even butch women. They do not even have to be consistent but can switch back and forth between masculine and feminine in dress, style and behavior, even from day to day. Men are much less free; departures from approved masculine behavior are savagely punished by society.[13] Social sanctions are much stronger and are sometimes backed up by the law. Until recently, male but not female homosexuality was punished by law even if in private between consenting adults. Despite reform, the male homosexual is still considerably restricted and harassed by the law in a way that lesbians have never been. A male transvestite can be arrested and punished if he tries to parade in his favorite silk stockings (they haven't moved with the times—tights are too masculine!) and spike-heel shoes. At a time when liberated women are burning bras, men lack the basic right to wear them. By contrast, a woman can stride down Threadneedle Street or Omonia Square in a three-piece suit, and according to the times, be regarded as fashionable or, at worst, eccentric. If she wishes she may don leather jacket and boots or a false beard and still remain within the law.

No woman is forced to take on the basic female role of maternity. Indeed, if any man tries to impose it on her against her will, he is liable to be prosecuted for rape. For a man to opt out of the distinctive male role of military service is extremely difficult. In Greece, such a man would be sent to prison for a long stretch; in America, draft dodgers have been forced to flee abroad. Even in Britain, conscientious objectors have been treated with great harshness, and the law has been backed up by the spiteful distribution of white feathers.

But the saddest figure of all, at least in Greece, is the cuckold. The man whose wife takes a lover suffers the derision and contempt of the entire society, and even his virility is called into question—the ultimate degradation for a Greek! A milder form of degradation is that of the henpecked husband. A man who beats his wife is regarded by society as a monster to be punished, and the wife as someone to be pitied; a man who is beaten by his wife is a figure of fun, a subject for ridicule. Even today we laugh at the thought of Xanthippe tipping a piss-pot over the great Socrates—the other way around, it would not be funny. The man cannot win either way: if he's brutal, he's punished; if he's submissive, he's laughed at.

Right from childhood men are prevented, in all aspects of life, from adopting female attitudes, female pursuits or female emotions. In Greece it would never do to see a man cry, and in England very few men can cry without feeling guilty afterward. So strong is the taboo against men's tears that were I to mention the names of some men who I know have cried, this would add tears of humiliated mortification to their earlier tears of distress —an Englishman in adversity is expected to keep smiling, retain a stiff upper lip and whistle to keep his courage up, all at the same time. Men not only feel shame at their own "lapses" into "effeminacy" but feel scorn and contempt for those who fail to be fully masculine. John Stuart Mill, assiduously quoted by Millett, writes of the Englishman: ". . . people are little aware . . . how early the notion of his inherent superiority to a girl arises in his mind; how it grows with his growth and strengthens with his strength; how it is inoculated by one schoolboy upon another; how early the youth thinks himself superior to his mother, owing her perhaps forbearance, but no real respect; and how sublime and sultan-like a sense of superiority he feels, above all, over the woman whom he honours by admitting her to a partnership of his life."[14]

It is as well to remember that Mill had a very odd childhood —he did not go to school but, up to adolescence, spent all his time at home.[15] He was hardly likely to know what the average schoolboy felt; he had never been one, never met any. The contempt that Mill believed men felt for women is in fact directed not at women but at effeminate men. Indeed, Mill himself may have been a victim of this attitude: "Stephen called him 'a book in breeches . . . as narrow as it was possible for a man to be and as cold as ice.' " Stephen thought Mill not so much cold-blooded as bloodless, a body stunted by brains, lacking in the fire and force of the fully grown male animal. Like some other innately robust characters of the time, he suspected a morbid streak of sentimentalism in Mill.[16]

This attitude toward men who are not "fully grown male animals" is a persecution that women who are not fully grown female animals do not have to face.

English friends talking to me about their childhood never recall having felt contempt for girls, but they do confess to having felt a "brutal superiority" to boys who seemed effeminate:

"When I was about eleven I remember going with my mates to an exhibition held to raise money for the school. For some reason they had hired a team of tap-dancers to amuse the people in the exhibition. They were all about our age, three girls and a boy—

he was dressed in a fluffy pullover and purple check trousers. We all felt hell's sorry for him having to do these antics on the stage in front of us all. We assumed he had a ghastly dominating mother who had pushed him into it. Afterwards, we met him in the hall and we all told him how sorry we felt that he had to dress up like that in public and cavort around in those silly shiny shoes. He didn't even see what we were getting at. He'd actually enjoyed being up there prancing around. That did it. We all cut him dead and walked off in silent contempt."

The contempt is not for feminine activities and characteristics as such, but for feminine activities and characteristics when found in men. In fact, effeminacy is a caricature rather than a simulation of femininity: it is not an attempt to appear feminine, but an attempt to appear unmasculine—an attempt to adopt a "camp" rather than a feminine role.[17] In a sense, men never despise femininity at all—the camp traits they mock are basically different from true femininity; after all, not many women have limp wrists or call their friends "ducky."

Germaine Greer devotes a whole chapter to the debasement of words used to describe women, most of which these days are confined to the Scrabble board. You could probably get up to sixty-three points for "slammerkin" or "rutabaga."[18] And Miss Greer fails to confess that any man could compile a list, as long as hers, which would indicate the debasement of the male, equally nastily. Is a woman ever called a bastard? "Nonsense" is dismissed as "cock" or "balls"—just the same degradation of the male."[19] In addition, the "failed" male has to face specific insults: queer, pansy, fairy, faggot, queen, fruit.

Kate Millett quotes survey data as showing that a large minority of women would prefer to have been born men and claims that this is especially true for young girls, "whereas boys overwhelmingly reject the option of being girls."[20] This, far from being an indictment of the girls' fate, reinforces all the other evidence that women have more choice than men: at the overt, articulated level, women can admit even a desire to change sex, whereas men rigorously repress any such thought and will not admit it to themselves, let alone to anyone else. Masculinity is acquired later in life and after a cross-sex identification;[21] it is less secure and it can be threatened in a way femininity cannot be. This is why it is defended more rigorously and why it is men, not women, who suffer from this: whatever men and women may say in questionnaires, when it comes to actual behavior far more men than women try to change their sex.[22] Male transexualism, a desire to be a female so strong that "he truly believes he is a female and hopes to have his body changed accordingly," is from three to eight times more common than female transexualism.[23] Whatever Women's Lib may say, few women share the sense of self-hatred and self-contempt of these men. The male transexual "has a disgust for his male genitalia which represent a constant reminder of his unwanted anatomic sex and he will with extraordinary perseverance seek surgery to give him female genitalia."[24]

Most men do not find their masculinity so unbearable that they wish to part with it! There are many more men for whom the sexual problems of masculinity are not unbearable but still a source of distress and anxiety. Even for the majority, the sexual aspects of masculinity are not entirely problem-free; fear of failure, of impotence, is a real, if covert, fear for many men: "In a sense a woman can never fail in bed . . . A woman is never impotent. Frigid yes, impotent, no. If she doesn't have an orgasm, we say, 'too bad' but we don't say 'you failed' . . . Ah, but pity the poor male! . . . Impotence is humiliatingly obvious . . . Every young boy is taught that a man is supposed to be 'masculine.' And as he becomes a teenager he learns, through gossip, reading, and the media, that every real man is expected to be a good sexual performer. A boy begins to wonder if he measures up . . . The man feels pressured to perform well and if the pressure is strong enough he may be so fearful and distracted that he will be unable to achieve an erection. A few episodes of this nature coupled with the man's concept of what society considers good sexual performance and he begins to think of himself as something less than a man."[25]

I have deliberately taken this description not from a book of psychiatric case histories, but from *The Sensuous Man*, a best seller on sexual technique rather than sexual problems and aimed at the male population at large. Impotence, or anxiety about it, is by its very nature a specifically male problem. Impotence can be paralleled by frigidity in women as a pathological condition, but occasional anxiety about impotence is widespread among fully potent men—and this is not paralleled by female anxiety about frigidity. There is a sharp dividing line between success and failure in normal men, but not in normal women. Because of this, men are more depressed by sexual problems than women: ". . . often man feels as though some Nemesis had suddenly befallen him: perhaps a doom merited by long-forgotten guilty thoughts or erections. One might expect the same reaction in women who have genital anaesthesia but although many of them are anxious people they are not so deeply affected as men."[26]

Frigidity and a lack of sexual desire may well be more closely correlated than is the case with impotence. Impotence can be experienced by men with strong sexual drive, and there can be no partial potency in the way that there can be partial frigidity with restricted but real enjoyment. It is for all these reasons that literature, from the erudite and obscure case histories of the psychiatrists to the agony columns of popular magazines, feature impotence and fear about it more than they feature frigidity. It is not, as Germaine Greer implies, because society as a matter of course takes men's problems more seriously than women's.[27]

It is Women's Libbers who are the discriminators; the problems of women are discussed incessantly, those of men ignored or mocked. Kate Millett sneers at Norman Mailer's preoccupation with "the male's own fears for his masculinity, his courage, his dominance, the test of erection."[28] But it is a test she will never have to meet. Mailer's heroes are anxious about sexual failure in a way that a woman need never be. Although their obsessional anxiety may be unrepresentative, Millett's gibes show a lack of insight and understanding to be expected only from a dogmatic and hostile purveyor of sexual politics. This dogmatism leads her to bigoted and wrong-headed interpretations of reality: "The penis . . . in both preliterate and civilized patriarchies is given the most crucial significance, the subject both of endless boasting and endless anxiety" only because it is the "badge of the male's superior status."[29] It would be much simpler to assume that man is anxious about the penis as a penis rather than as a badge—worried about his sexuality rather than about his "superior status." But of one thing we can be sure: Miss Millett will always reject a simple explanation in favor of one that is complex, intricate, obscure and wrong.

She also has a unique gift of taking a simple truth and exaggerating and distorting it until it becomes an absurdity: "All male activity, maleness, perhaps patriarchy itself, depends upon penile erection: 'Here it is that mastery and domination, the central capacity of the man's sexual nature must meet acceptance or fail.' To achieve erection the man must be master."[30] To achieve erection, gaining and giving sexual satisfaction and enjoyment, the man need not be master, but he must have overcome any fears and doubts about the aggressive element in his sexuality. "Male sexuality, because of the primitive necessity of pursuit and penetration, does contain an important element of aggressiveness; an element which is both recognized and responded to by the female who yields and submits. Moreover, it is impossible for the male human who is frightened of women either himself to become fully aroused or to awake a corresponding response in the female. Impotence in men whether partial or complete is invariably the result of fears which may be and often are unconscious."[31] Reports of impotence among males with domineering female partners confirm the need for the male to accept the inherently dominant element in his sexuality,[32] unchallenged by the forces of female liberators.

Kate Millett's attempt to deny and ridicule the aggressive aspect of sexuality potentially undermines a factor that is necessary to sexual pleasure for both men and women. Our world involves aggressiveness without hostility; the Women's Lib world, hostility without aggressiveness: it is a world in which insecure men and unsatisfied women share only a hostile indifference to each other.

In our society the man is expected to initiate, the woman to accept or encourage, to reject or discourage. This creates problems for the atypically aggressive woman or the atypically passive man. But encouragement is such an open-ended concept that there is scope for all but the most butch women to play the game successfully within the very elastic rules; the plight of the passive man is far worse, for unless he is fortunate enough to be sought out by the aggressive woman, he is unlikely ever to establish a relationship at all.

Germaine Greer gives us a pitiful sketch of the woman as sexual decoy "waiting for the telephone to ring."[33] She does not see that there is an equal anxiety for the man who faces the dilemma of deciding whether to ring that same telephone, whether to take the very real risk of being rejected rudely, coldly or with false effusiveness and obviously invented excuses.

The Women's Libbers' attack on supposed female passivity is closely related to their attack on women's treatment as sex objects—a treatment that they regard as extremely degrading. It is difficult to see both why they regard it as degrading, and more important, why they neglect the fact that men are sex objects just as much. In terms of external appearance, men are becoming equally preoccupied with the effect that their hair, their clothes, even their eau de Cologne, will have on women. This is not entirely a new phenomenon, for aristocracies have always had their male dandies. Louis XIV, Beau Brummell, Samuel Pepys and even Kaiser Bill himself paid vast attention to their looks and their dress, and the Byronic Romantics were the *hommes fatales* of their age.

But the syndrome of men as sex objects does not end here. The *machismo* cult of which men are victims is another far more destructive and oppressive side of it; there is no equivalent for women. In Greece the victims are much more numerous: for a Greek victim of this toughness cult, taking a girl out can be a hazardous matter, especially if he is obsessed with proving his own virility and outfighting every man who dares to stare at his girl or even glance at her indirectly. Even in England there seems to be a whole population of hundred-pound weaklings who are forever having sand kicked in their face by the local beach bully until they take a course with Charles Atlas. There may be a big market in cosmetics for women, but there is also an impressive trade in chest expanders, dumbbells, Indian clubs and punching bags for men. The professional male sex object, such as the boxer, sinks far lower than Miss World; which is more degrading —parading in a scanty costume in front of glassy-eyed, mesmerized males or battering another human being into insensibility? Who comes off worse, the loser of a beauty contest or a punch-drunk old heavyweight, a chopping block for the new champions?

As far as Miss World is concerned, there is something much worse than being a sex object, and that is having a fixation on a sex object. It is sad that men should idolize pinups, beauty queens, models, but it is much sadder for the men than for the objects. Men's tendency to get fixated on distant or even ludicrous sex objects can become tragic if this is projected onto fetishistic objects rather than females. It is preferable that men seek sex objects in women rather than in high-heeled shoes, rubber hot-water bottles, plastic raincoats or frogmen's suits! Women at least stick to pop stars or Joe Namath.

Men's aggressiveness is used by society in its armed forces, which provide the only examples of jobs that are totally and entirely reserved for men. Women may play support roles in the army as clerks or drivers, cooks or parachute packers, but they are never used as combat troops.[34] This is a grotesque inequality between the sexes that Women's Lib rarely attacks. They wish to be stockbrokers and bus drivers, cameramen and surgeons but not, it would seem, fighter pilots or paratroopers, snipers or naval gunners, commandos or tank captains. They do not particularly wish these jobs to be open to them, and they certainly do not wish to be liable for conscription into them. As usual, their wish for liberation is restricted to the pleasanter, more glamorous side of masculine roles.

But if women are to be fully liberated, then either they must be equally liable for military service or else all the armed forces must be abolished. If, as Germaine Greer suggests, all employers should "show an equal distribution of men and women in all parts of their enterprise,"[35] this applies to the army as well as the networks, to the air force as well as the airlines, to the navy as well as the engineering industry. Equal numbers in the forces can only be achieved either by conscripting women or by having neither men nor women as fighters.

A demand for emancipation, rather than liberation, does not involve these absurd changes. It recognizes the innate differences between men and women that disqualify women from certain jobs such as combat roles in the army. Women are not as strong as men and are constitutionally less aggressive.[36] Even in mechanized and remote warfare, there is still a need for hard physical slogging by the infantry, as the Americans have recently found to their cost. Women as combat troops would also be a liability to the army, and because of their "regrettable" tendency to become pregnant, a female malingerer would always escape the fighting by this simple method.

The one military role that women are sometimes given is that of last-ditch defender of the children when all the men are killed and the direct threat to her offspring induces counteraggression in the mother. The division of labor between mothers and soldiers is a necessary and sensible one. It is possible to *imagine* a society where this division was made along a dimension orthogonal to the division between the sexes, so that half the women were fighters and half child-minders, and the men were divided up likewise. But such a selection would have to be made early if the two groups were to be brought up for these divergent roles.

If it were made early, it could not be made on the basis of proven aptitude but would be arbitrary—certainly more arbitrary than the present selection on the basis of sex. As male aggressive behavior has had adaptive and survival value in the past, it is clear that selection by sex correlates fairly well to the innate tendencies of men and women, and certainly gives better results than an arbitrary process.

There are strong demographic reasons why a nation dare not put its women in an army fighting at the front. If a society loses a large number of men in a war it can, if it wishes, make up the population losses in one generation by legalizing polygamy, as the Mormons did in Utah after losing many of their men in a battle with the Indians and with other white Americans, or the Germans did after the Thirty Years' War,[37] or by encouraging illegitimate breeding as the Paraguayans did after losing half their male population in wars with Bolivia, Brazil, Argentina and Uruguay. If the Paraguayans had lost half their women, then their society would have been permanently crippled. For these reasons, women's lives are never risked in war as often as men's, even when there are heavy civilian casualties. Among most mammals, social organization is centered around this need to preserve and protect the females, and the male has evolved into the fighter, the defender, the hunter.

One expression of men's desire to protect women that enrages Women's Lib is chivalry. Kate Millett as usual falls back on Mill: "With an admirable touch of candour, Mill admits that no man would wish for himself the conditions of life he chivalrously consigns to women; the pastoral coign of a Queen's garden would appal any man confined to it . . ."[38]

It is difficult to see why Mill, a partisan of Millett's views, should need candor or be forced to "admit"—this is hardly a reluctant concession dragged from a male chauvinist. Whether a man would prefer a life in a "garden" depends on where he is and what he is faced with. A Queen's garden is better than a King's war. Men serving in the First World War often longed to leave the slaughter of the trenches for the comfort and security of a garden.[39] When the army officers in *Journey's End*[40] escape for a time from their bunker in conversation and reminiscence, it is their gardens they seek, their lawns and hedges, trees and flowers; even Trotter, the promoted private from Birmingham, dreams of his little garden. The war in Flanders was an extreme case, but many men faced with aggression, strain, competition must share his longing to escape to the pastoral scene that Millett derides. When Mill wrote, he could safely avoid the world of mud and gas, shrapnel and shell shock, early death and hideous wounds that the male may undergo, because he lived in the security of Pax Britannica. It was as remote from him as it is from many Women's Libbers in the era of nuclear stalemate. The peace in our time is no more inevitably guaranteed to last than that which Mill knew. The chances that it will last are greater. But who would have predicted such "post-atomic" wars as Korea, Vietnam, Biafra or Bangladesh? Who would have predicted the degree of British military involvement in Northern Ireland? Women's Lib complains incessantly of the self-sacrifice of women. War memorials in every town and village proclaim a different kind of sacrifice, and one that is not exacted from women. No doubt, if Women's Lib gets its way, cenotaphs to the bearer of the Unknown Soldier will spring up all over the world.

Chivalry today is not based on any real need to protect women from physical danger, although even in peacetime our lives are not completely devoid of a need for the physical courage and sacrifice of men. There are fires in which firemen die, bank robberies in which guards or policemen are shot, shipwrecks that endanger the lives of local lifeboatmen. Today, perhaps thanks to Women's Lib, we are apt to laugh at incidents like the sinking of H.M.S. *Birkenhead* carrying soldiers and their families:[41] the women and children were given the available space in the ship's boats, while the men stood at attention as the ship sank. We laugh, but what are we to replace it with? Are we to demand in true Women's Lib style, "Women the boats, men and children first"?

The everyday chivalry of men, however, is qualitatively different—it is an anachronism if judged in terms of real physical needs; it is inauthentic if judged in terms of "authentic" indispensable necessities for the survival of the species. It is only a legacy of such one-time real needs; today it is based on a myth. But then, what is wrong with myths? The place of mythology in the field of politics has been well established—no less by socialists than by right-wingers. Why not make mythology respectable in the field of personal relations as well? Why not perpetuate a myth that leads to pleasure and satisfaction? When a man moves to the other side, by the curb, I do not feel grateful because he is protecting me from the "lethal" dangers of the road; I feel a tinge of warm feeling because, however ritualistic and mechanical the gesture, however superficial the acquaintance or relationship, his gesture has effected a momentary link. No doubt a liberated woman would shout "male chauvinist pig" and elbow him into the gutter. When a man offers me his coat or jacket if I'm cold, carries my bags if I'm tired, or walks me home if it's dark, it is not the protection or comfort that he gives that are the essence—it is the pleasant feeling that I get from the recognition of a "care gesture" and the pleasant feeling that he gets from the knowledge that the gesture will be recognized. It is the same feeling that I got when I was told on the phone by a friend who was away: "Take care of yourself until I come back! After that, I'll take care of you." The fact that we both knew that I was perfectly capable of taking care of myself and that I was unlikely to die of starvation or be attacked by Red Indians didn't make the euphoric feeling any less real.

For Women's Lib, chivalry is a vast male conspiracy to keep oppressed women quiet and happy. For me, and I am sure for the majority of women who have not been brainwashed into feeling too guilty to admit it, chivalry is a pleasure, a game—it is fun and we want it to stay.

The difference in innate aggressiveness, women's "tendency" to become pregnant and, in extreme cases of total conventional warfare, the demographic reasons are not the only explanations why women are not included among combat troops.

The army depends on strong bonds of loyalty and comradeship between the men if its morale is to be maintained. If there were "mixed" fighting units which included women, the strong sexual attractions between couples would set up intensely disruptive tensions and jealousies that could never arise in civilian job situations, not subject to the special conditions of discipline, hierarchical structure and intense loyalty inherent in the army.

Women are excluded for the same reason that homosexuality is feared.[42] Millett looks at male loyalties and comradeship with her usual mechanical sneer. Regardless of the context in which an army is used and for whatever purpose, she presumably wishes to abolish the military and masculinity together, for she is vituperative against both: "Much of the glamorization of masculine comradery in warfare originates in what one might designate 'the men's house sensibility.' Its sadistic and brutalizing aspects are disguised in military glory and a particularly cloying species of masculine sentimentality."[43] She develops this theme at great length in a long attack on the militarism and male supremacism of Nazi Germany,[44] from which we are presumably expected to conclude that all armies and all male comradeship are evil and dispensable. Yet who does she think defeated the Nazis? If the men of England, of Greece, of Russia, of America had not had some of the qualities of soldiers, of traditional masculinity, we would have lost the war. The price of victory over the extreme male militarism of the Nazis was a share of these values in the other societies. An army recruited from Millett's Utopia would have been smashed by the Germans, the society destroyed and an ultramasculine tyranny imposed. If the democracies are not to be attacked and defeated (as they nearly were in 1939–1945) by extreme male supremacist societies, they must preserve some masculine values, attitudes and institutions. We need not imitate the militarism of the Kaiser or the Nazis, of Tojo or the Soviet Union, but we need to maintain the much despised, basic masculinity if we are to withstand them. The parallel between the views of some Women's Libbers and the pacifists of the 1930s is a curiously close one. Although the threat from Hitler grew, English pacifists vehemently opposed rearmament, and as a result Britain entered the war with too few tanks and too few aircraft.[45] For the first two years Britain was hard pressed, but as the British showed, it is possible to repair a deficiency in armaments fairly quickly. But what if the British people's very ability and willingness to fight back had been destroyed by social changes of the kind urged by Women's Lib? Courage and fighting spirit, loyalty and comradeship cannot be created as quickly as mere armaments. General and complete disarmament and an end to war would be a fine achievement, and the abolition of masculinity would achieve this even more effectively than abolishing weapons. But unilateral abolition of masculinity suffers from the same drawbacks as unilateral disarmament.

The Women's Libbers' ambivalence to the army extends to other aspects of the man's world. They cannot decide whether they want to become men or destroy them. One reason for the confusion is the split of the masculine world into a "good boy's" culture and a "bad boy's" culture—and males must submit to both. It is a split which causes immense problems for boys and men and especially for adolescents—a split which women are lucky to avoid. The female culture of our society is strong and confident; it is society's official moral order. Male culture is divided. There is the official morality but there is also pressure to be tough, to be a "man with balls," a "bad-ass nigger."[46] These are not reinforcing ways of oppressing women, as Women's Lib asserts; if men's primary concern was with oppressing women in this way, they would have taken good care to present a united front. As it is, these two moralities have the effect of dividing men; men and their heroes are split into "good men" and admired bad men: Al Capone, Billy the Kid, Robin Hood, Dick Turpin. Men feel torn apart inside by conflicting pressures, women have a much more united outlook. The heroines of history and even more so of today, whether typical or atypical women, do not present the same problem of ambivalence. Women are the carriers of society's values. Men are deviant in the sense that many of the qualities admired in them are also ones that society has to regard with disapproval. A man who is a "helluva good guy" is not altogether respectable. He is a likable scoundrel, but nonetheless a scoundrel. The bachelor subculture of drink, gambling, irregular hours and fighting is jokingly admired by men, but they are also forced to abjure it.

Women's Lib portrays society and morality as a male invention to coerce and punish women. However, many men see it exactly the other way around. Though there is no Men's Lib to express their feelings of being downtrodden, many are bitter about it in conversation. One man I interviewed said, "Society is a woman who enjoys punishing men. The typical 'bad' person in society is young and male, the typical 'good' person is female and middle-aged, a Mrs. Roosevelt, a Carrie Nation, or a Margaret Sanger. Women are a virtuous group seeking to impose their moral standards on men." American women led by the Women's Christian Temperance Union imposed Prohibition on the American men. In most countries, women are treated more leniently by the law than men. Corporal punishment for women has very often been abolished long before it has ended for men, and even where capital punishment is still used, women convicted of capital crimes are less likely to be executed. In Britain, even when a woman does commit a crime, she is more likely to be cautioned by the police and less likely to be prosecuted than a man.[47] Apart from crimes committed in order to sustain drug dependence, most serious crimes are committed by young men. Young women figure very unimportantly in such statistics. In Britain, the rebuilding of Holloway women's prison has been strenuously opposed by wide sections of the press and the public because it seems increasingly unnecessary to have a large prison for female offenders, both because the number who commit serious crimes is so small and because most experts believe that prison is even less effective in dealing with women than it is with men.

The most harshly treated of all deviants, considering how harmless many of them are, are male sexual perverts.[48] Here the double standard works in reverse with a vengeance. "Flashers" are charged with "indecent exposure with intent to insult a female"; women who strip in public, like the nudes outside No. 10 Downing Street, are not treated anywhere near so severely. Peeping Toms, like the exhibitionists, are often timid people, but even when they do not attack or molest their victims,[49] they are viciously punished by courts of local vigilantes. Society is extreme in its rejection of these inadequates. They get heavy jail sentences, and when in jail, have to be protected from other prisoners.[50] Similarly, although, according to Lord Devlin, a pimp does not exploit a prostitute any more than an agent exploits an actress,[51] the pimp is far more savagely treated: in Western European countries, prostitutes are fined, pimps go to jail, and again, they may be attacked by other prisoners. In the interwar period, special legislation was brought in to deal severely with pimps, even to the extent of flogging them.

The image painted by Women's Lib—men always at the top, men in all privileged positions in society—is an extremely lopsided one, as the examples of men as deviants, as addicts or as cannon fodder make clear. I have deliberately stressed the more unhappy side of men's lives, the harsher treatment they often receive, because of a real need to right the balance, to complete the picture and present men in a less glamorous but also less distorted way, a way that should divest the Women's Libbers' delusions of persecution and oppression from their remaining plausibility—after all, the "oppressors" are often more deprived than the "oppressed"! Some of men's misfortunes are thrust on them, others are a result of the naturally greater variability of men,[52] and yet others stem from society's greater willingness to allow men to sink further; the greater pressure on men to succeed means that some men fail the more disastrously. For all these reasons, the outcasts of society are nearly all male—crime is predominantly a male activity,[53] most sexual offenders are male, most of the tramps and derelicts are male. Far more men than women are to be found in reception centers, common lodging houses or even sleeping rough.[54]

It is far too facile to blame the stereotypes for all of men's misfortunes. A lot of them may be shared by women when our emancipation is complete; the truth is that the opening up of greater opportunities to succeed is accompanied by access to greater "opportunities" to fail. Recognition of this does not weaken the case for emancipation, but it does mean that a greater proportion of women will be found among the ranks of inadequates; this has to be predicted and anticipated as an inevitable concomitant of emancipation and should not be shrugged off and evaded. The problems of emancipation are at least predictable, finite and bearable. The problems of liberation are, by contrast, unpredictable, immense and unacceptable, and this is why Women's Lib is not willing to face up to the negative aspects of the greater adoption of male roles by women. They demand not merely equality of opportunity for women but equality of performance for men and women in *all* spheres; this would mean the artificial retardation of women in some fields, and in others the pressurization and even the conscription of women into occupations for which they are clearly not suited. If, for example, women police officers were regularly and frequently faced with the necessity of pursuing armed criminals or evicting drunken laborers from bars, they would find this a much greater strain than their male colleagues. It is one thing to urge that women be allowed equal access to male occupations, it is quite another to suggest that they should as a matter of "right" be subject to the same competitive pressures. Emancipation, coupled with an improved status for the role of wife and mother and the preservation of rational differences in the upbringing of boys and girls, would give women a much wider choice in the life style they adopt and would protect them from the strain and insecurity that men inevitably face. A man who is not successful in his occupation has no alternative sense of self-esteem open to him, and his upbringing often makes it impossible for him to face the thought of continued failure—a failure in the eyes of his associates, a failure in his own estimation of himself. Suicide, addiction, a decision to drop out altogether may be the chosen and yet, in a way, predetermined alternative.

The case for Men's Lib is, if anything, a stronger one than that for Women's Lib, but it is untenable for physiological reasons. As Prime Minister Golda Meir—who has two children and six grandchildren—said, "Women's Lib is just a lot of foolishness. It's the men who are discriminated against. They can't bear children. And no one's likely to do anything about that."[55] The case for women's emancipation, however, has a parallel where men are concerned. Men should have a right to get away from the toughness, aggression and virility syndrome if they wish to. The two legal constraints of conscription and persecution of homosexuals have been abolished in England. But this is not the case in most other countries; these coercive restrictions are so unfair to men that they should rank on a par with equality of opportunity and pay for women, as basic social rights, in all countries.

For both men and women there is no need to abolish sexual stereotypes, as Women's Lib asserts, but there is a need to loosen the connections between the various aspects of masculinity, in the same way that there is a need to make femininity less monolithic. A man can be virile without having to take on the cult of toughness and *machismo;* he should be presented with an assemblage of *male* qualities and be able to choose from them the way in which he will express his masculinity, without being forced to adopt the whole package.

The Liberated Woman?
... and Her Liberators

The Women's Lib movement is like the army of a small Latin-American dictatorship—all generals and no privates. There may be mute, inglorious Milletts and village Greers in the background, but they are firmly kept there and treated with utter condescension by the leadership. The leaders do not merely despise the unliberated but extend their contempt to their own "liberated" rank and file. Germaine Greer: "In England, Women's Liberation Workshops are appearing in the suburban haunts of the educated housewife, and in the universities. There is no great coherence in their theory and no particular imagination or efficiency to be observed in their methods."[1]

Women's Libbers are obsessionally proud of the loose structure of their movement—there are no officials, no formal representatives, no definite institutions[2]—*ad hoc ad nauseam.* In "liberated" theory this structure should free the members; in practice it frees the leaders. Leadership goes by default to the most flamboyant spokeswomen of the day—neither responsible nor accountable to anyone, with no mandate and no constraints to shape their statements and actions. This absence of structure is only possible because Women's Lib is not a people's movement;

it is an eclectic sect drawn from the trendier section of the middle classes.[3] It is because of this peculiarly narrow membership base and inchoate organization that Women's Lib concentrates on trivial, glamorous targets and uses tactics aimed at gaining publicity rather than results. Sally Oppenheim clearly demonstrated this when she recently contrasted the Women's Lib obsession with the Miss World contest with their neglect of the far more important but mundane and difficult work of practical reform.[4] While Sally Oppenheim was working for the abolition, as the basis for legal assessment of damages, of the widow's chances of remarriage—a system which gives the court the right to fix payment on its own evaluation of the plaintiff's physical charms— Women's Libbers were out disrupting a beauty contest by throwing cabbages at Bob Hope. They didn't even manage to hit him —tending to prove that they have not, after all, liberated themselves from women's inability to throw straight. There were no Women's Libbers demonstrating outside the courts where genuinely degrading beauty assessments were going on, and where the women assessed had little choice as to whether they were there or not.

The Women's Lib movement, in its anxiety to avoid the oligarchic structures predicted by Robert Michels for any political organization,[5] has succumbed to the tyranny of charismatic leadership. Michels ended up supporting Mussolini as Il Duce, the great leader who incorporated in his person all the wishes and aspirations of the Italian people. By default or design, Women's Lib has become a cult that only expresses itself through the person of whoever happens to be the current "liberated" celebrity. In America, Gloria Steinem is Women's Lib—the cult figure is the movement. Some members of local Women's Lib groups are resentful of the excessive prominence of the Milletts, the Steinems and the Greers, but as there is no structure, there can be no way of dethroning them. There is nothing to bridge the gap between the best sellers written by the leadership and the scrubby little broadsheets produced in the local "workshops"—

between the booming, divine, unchallenged voice of the famous leaders and the impotent squeaking of the local shrews. Every liberated household has its *Female Eunuch,* but *Shrew,* according to Germaine Greer herself, never gets beyond the boundaries of Tufnel Park.[6]

It is essential to look closely at the leaders of the liberated, not only because they are the very incarnation of the movement but also because they are the chief prototype we have of the brave new liberated woman of the future. It would be unfair to select the really way-out extremists—Valerie Solanas of the Society for Cutting Up Men, whose manifesto states: "Scum will kill all men who are not in the men's auxiliary of Scum[7]. . . The few remaining men can live out their puny days dropped out on drugs or strutting around in drag or . . . they can go off to the nearest friendly neighbourhood suicide centre where they will be quietly, quickly and painlessly gassed to death";[8] or, on a milder but equally eccentric note Martha Shelley, the radical lesbian, who proclaims that "Lesbianism is one road to freedom—freedom from oppression by men[9]. . . Lesbianism involves love between women. Isn't love between equals healthier than sucking up to an oppressor?"[10]—all sentiments which would undoubtedly be endorsed by Jill Johnston and other radical lesbian luminaries.

Such perverse perspectives are so obviously outside the realm of the possible and the desirable that they can only be regarded as comic entertainment. Women's Lib can only be fairly undermined by attacking the best of its advocates, by concentrating on the work of such considerable scholars as Germaine Greer or Kate Millett.

As leaders of Women's Liberation, the Greers and the Milletts must, *par excellence,* be assumed to be liberated from the stereotype that they claim society has foisted on women—the view of women as illogical, unable to think quantitatively, ignorantly dogmatic. In fact, it is time the liberators liberated themselves; the irony is that those characteristics they attack as the hallmarks of the "unliberated" female are found to an alarmingly marked degree in their books. If their books were given to an intelligent unprejudiced male, we should not be surprised if on this evidence alone, he came to the conclusion that women did think in a muddled, illogical way. They have, in fact, done their sex a disservice.

All the manifestations of muddled, illogical thinking—inconsistency, circular argument, false antithesis, false extrapolation, bending the meanings of words, special pleading—all these can be found prolifically in the writings of the intellectual leaders of Women's Lib. Kate Millett has a spectacular penchant for self-justifying argument not seen since the days of *The Good Soldier Schweik:* ". . . many women do not recognize themselves as discriminated against; no better proof could be found of the totality of their conditioning."[11] The much more straightforward explanation—that absence of recognition reflects an absence of reprehensible discrimination—did not occur to her, or if it did, it has been suppressed in the interests of keeping her rigid ideology intact. This is not an isolated example, for later she writes: "Perhaps nothing is so depressing an index of the inhumanity of the male-supremacist mentality as the fact that the more genial human traits are assigned to the underclass: affection, response to sympathy, kindness, cheerfulness. There are a host of what would be termed 'nutritive' feminine functions here which it appears the male has ascribed to the female because he disregards their value and utility in himself . . ."[12] Once again Millett has wriggled out of an uncomfortable fact by distorting reality. Once again, truth is treated as another form of exploitation by "them against us." Millett's difficulty is that society ascribes to women the most humane values and virtues; this is starkly incompatible with her view of women as despised and rejected. To solve this contradiction and save her theory intact, she misrepresents men's attitudes to these qualities and invents the unlikely notion that society does not value these qualities intrinsically or respect them in men as well as women. Do we really not prefer a kind or cheerful man to a callous or gloomy one? Quite unnecessarily she also drags into this argument her view of women as an underclass: she postulates[13] that women and underclasses in general have these genial qualities assigned to them—her imagination is peopled with sympathetic slaves, affectionate peasants and kindly laborers who all flock to the rescue of her argument that nutritive qualities are contemptuously assigned to the underclasses. In fact, historically, the "top dogs," far from inevitably assigning genial qualities to the "underclasses," are just as likely to regard them as being brutal, sullen and coarse.

The curious view of causality held by the Women's Libbers is best illustrated in that happy hunting ground for pretentiousness, *The Female Eunuch:* "Perhaps the pop revolution which has replaced sentiment with lust by forcibly incorporating the sexual ethos of black urban blues into the culture created by the young for themselves has had a far-reaching effect on sexual *mores.*"[14] "The young have a culture created . . . for themselves," yet "the pop revolution," seen as something external and apart from this culture, has "forcibly" determined its sexual ethos. It is a remarkable attempt to reconcile contradictions, to have both free will and determinism on her side. This is a general characteristic of Women's Libbers' writings and thinking. They see the vast majority of women as entirely manipulated, completely at the mercy of social pressures, and yet they themselves are fully immune from these allegedly all-pervasive forces. The actions, feelings and beliefs of all other women are predetermined, the result of cultural conditioning—free will is reserved for the liberated élite.

The most common flaw in the arguments of the Women's Libbers is their tendency to discern false antitheses where none exist, and to draw spurious conclusions by false extrapolation from one society to another. Millett's attack on Freud epitomizes this flaw: "Freud responded to Mill by arguing that the sexes are inherently different in temperament, and then, despite the logical contradiction, by deploring changes in upbringing which might erode these differences."[15] This false antithesis is a product of the liberators' total inability to grasp the logic of a multi-causal situation.[16] Freud asserts that the sexes are inherently different in temperament, *not* (as Millett infers) that innate factors are the exclusive cause of the differences seen in any one particular society. The truth is that both inherent factors and cultural influences determine the observed differences between the sexes. The Women's Lib argument amounts to saying that because cultural influences have been proved to be significant, inherent factors cannot possibly be a real cause of these differences. The opponents of Women's Lib–type ideologies do not regard the inherent differences that exist between the sexes as identical with the differences observed in any particular society at any particular time; society undoubtedly does exaggerate or minimize these innate differences. Today's sophisticated unisex fashions mark one end of the spectrum; the exaggerated masculinity of the sweat-and-sawdust gun-toting Mexican with his submissive and homebound female mark the other. We have a real but limited choice of the degree to which we foster or hinder these differences; we have no choice about their existence and we cannot eliminate them altogether.

Freud's claim is that if we depart too far in our behavior from our inherent selves, we face severe psychological problems. Millett's claim is that we can choose any kind of relationship between the sexes, including identical sex roles, and graft it onto all the individuals in society, without any adverse effects on the "graftees." Freud stresses the power of the subconscious—a part of the mind not so easily bludgeoned into line by the convictions of the liberated. The nervous disorders of a civilization reflect the strain between the demands of our social roles and our inherent selves —the greater the gap, the more acute the problem.[17] This central argument in Freud's theory accounts for his fear that the effect of changes in upbringing would be to erode the differences of temperament between men and women at one level, and so take them further away from their essential nature.

The Women's Lib tendency to argue from false antitheses

would not be so important if it only affected peripheral issues and arguments, but, in fact, their whole case is based upon this technique. The Women's Libbers believe that everybody adheres to one of two irreconcilable models of the world: there are those who see the sexes as inevitably occupying roles that are in all senses complementary opposites, and there are the liberated ones who believe that the sexes are essentially identical and that their roles should be indistinguishable from each other.[18] Anyone who has not liberated himself from logic and common sense can immediately see that there are, in fact, a very large number of intermediate positions that the individual can adopt which involve greater or lesser degrees of difference between the sexes. In the same way, the individual is not trapped in a dichotomy about the reform of sex roles in society. He is not forced, as Women's Lib implies, to choose between defending in a die-hard fashion the conventional sex roles actually existing in his society and supporting a move to integrate the separate sex cultures out of existence.

Anyone who has thought about sex roles has views about them at three levels: how they are now, what their innate tendency is, and how they ought to be. Women's Libbers seem to believe that the opponents of liberation are an undifferentiated, unenlightened mass who believe that the answers to these three questions coincide in the status quo. Once again, they set up a false dichotomy between this unenlightened belief pattern and a belief in the ideology of liberation. Once again, they blatantly betray the infinite subtleties of reality, in the interests of blunt antitheses. This artificial dichotomy has two functions: it sets up a caricature of the opposition's views which is much easier to demolish, and it justifies a faith in apocalyptic liberation, since the opposition's ideology is so monolithic, so unyielding that no reform is possible without a total conflict.

The Women's Lib characteristic antithesis between the real world of harsh total separation and the millenarian ideal of total fusion is implicit in Germaine Greer's extraordinary genetic argument: "of forty-eight chromosomes *only* one is different."[19] But is there a complete separation of male and female? Does a man in the Western world of the twentieth century need to be reminded and upbraided: Hath not a woman eyes? hath not a woman hands, organs, dimensions, senses, affections, passions? fed with the same food, hurt with the same weapons, subject to the same diseases, healed by the same means, warmed and cooled by the same winter and summer as a man is?[20]

The genetic argument in Germaine Greer's statement is no less absurd, based on the idea that a difference of one chromosome out of forty-eight means that one forty-eighth part of men and women is different! The chromosomes, in fact, do not operate as independent units but have an interacting effect.[21] Every cell in the human body is indelibly stamped male or female by the existence of the one different chromosome.[22] It is that very society which is supposed to separate men and women that chooses to treat them as equal human beings despite the fact that they are constructed of entirely different cells. Even the French think *vive l'humanité* as often as they think *vive la différence!*[23]

Occasionally Women's Libbers manage to progress beyond false antithesis to the superior realm of false extrapolation. They actually compare the position of women in different societies and recognize that social differences are not best analyzed in terms of antithetical absolutes. They devote a great deal of attention to societies in which women were, or are, abominably treated, and provide a nice warm feeling of horror and moral indignation for their liberated readers. Privileged women in industrial societies can gasp at the status of their sisters in Saudi Arabia, Tokugawa Japan, Sicily (but not Calabria!), Afghanistan and Nazi Germany.[24] Fair enough. The moral drawn from all this is that women are vastly happier and more fulfilled in the industrial societies of the West, where there is formal equality of the sexes and a narrowing of the differences in their life experience, than in the more traditional patriarchies that they have rightly calumnied. Fair enough. They then extrapolate from this comparison to their ideal, liberated world, where the sexes are forced to be identical in all respects, where the already limited gap between men and women has closed to nothing. And this is not fair enough. It just is not possible to extrapolate social changes in this simplistic, linear manner. There is no reason why a change that has undisputably had beneficial effects should continue to do so if extended indefinitely. The doubts that have recently been voiced about the need to drive for faster and even more splendid economic growth in affluent industrial societies clearly point to the fallacy in this style of argument.

Sexual pleasure is one of the many aspects of life that improves for women with a move away from a rigid and total division between the sexes. Sex is more fun for the couple who can share other interests and pleasures than for a couple whose worlds are as separate as those of a Castleford coal miner and his wife.[25] It does not follow from this that sex would be even more fun for the couple that has achieved the supreme liberated state of identical sex roles. The unyielding woman and the overgentle, timid man of such a Utopia might well find a lack of vitality and excitement in their total liberation, a liberation hardly compatible with the nature of the sex act itself.[26]

The Women's Libbers' weakness for false antithesis and unjustified extrapolation, and their difficulty in comprehending multicausal situations, can all be related to their inability to think quantitatively, or to appreciate the nature and results of scientific inquiry. In fact, they display all the weaknesses that society allegedly inculcates in women. For Kate Millett there is a "generally operative division between 'masculine' and 'feminine' subject matter, assigning the humanities and certain social sciences (at least in their lower or marginal branches) to the female—and science and technology, the professions, business and engineering to the male."[27] It is hard to see how the Libbers can reconcile their eagerness to enter these "important and prestigious" male preserves with their total inability and unwillingness to understand these key areas they want to be liberated into. I partly share their inability and unwillingness to understand statistics or the sciences, but not being, and not wishing to be, a liberated woman, I am not under the same moral obligation to master them.

It is illuminating to note the "unliberated" deficiencies of such a liberated book as Kate Millett's *Sexual Politics*. Clearly absent from this book is the language of quantities. Not only are there no statistics, tables, graphs or diagrams—the only numbers in the book are the page numbers—but there is no attempt at either a verbal analysis involving quantitative relationships or changes. Even the simple concepts of "bigger than" and "smaller than" are largely absent. There is no serious discussion of the role of science, technology or economic forces as factors shaping the changes in women's position that she dismisses; there is no attempt to apply a knowledge of the sciences to the fundamental question "What are the innate differences between men and women?"

Since Kate Millett has been kind enough to append to her book an enormously long list of the works she has diligently consulted, it is possible to give a detailed breakdown of the evidence on which she bases her case.[28]

Works Consulted by Kate Millett

	FIELDS	NUMBERS	
"Hard" Human Sciences	Biology	7	15
	Psychology (excluding psychoanalysis)	8	
"Soft" Human Sciences	Psychoanalysis	29	92
	Anthropology	29	
	Sociology	34	
Arts	History, etc.	76	200
	Literature	124	

What clearly emerges from this is what is obvious also from a careful reading of the book: it is an immensely erudite and scholarly work. It is precisely because of this that Kate Millett's total neglect of the more precise human sciences is so remarkable. Fundamental to Millett's entire argument is the conviction that there are no important innate differences between the sexes. Sometimes this is explicitly asserted, sometimes it is implicitly assumed—but it is always there. Surely such a central assumption should have been rigorously subjected to the test of empirical and scientific findings. Yet Kate Millett consulted three times as many sources on Genet as she did on biology, five times as many on Miller and Mailer as she did on experimental psychology. It may well be that she finds Norman Mailer more fascinating than boring old biology, than the complex effects of sex hormones on behavior or the production of conditioned reflexes in babies. If this is the case, then her book can fairly be regarded as an interesting exercise in recondite literary criticism, but hardly as a comprehensive analysis of the main issues involved in Women's Liberation. Not serious enough to be scientific, it is a fine example of the new, heavy *belles lettres* of the *salon* or the more sophisticated drawing room. It certainly wins a prize for humorless diligence and methodical thoroughness, but ultimately tells us little about women, nature or society.

Where Kate Millett eschews the use of statistics, Germaine Greer plunges inaccurately into them. Talking of comparative female crime rates she writes: "In 1854 . . . women were a quarter of all the people committed for trial on criminal charges; in this vintage year [1972] of female delinquency women will be less than 6 per cent of all admissions to prison."[29] She manages to get a striking comparison by comparing two totally different sets of statistics. She compares women committed for trial with those going to jail, ignoring the fact that many of those tried are acquitted and many of those convicted do not go to jail. In particular, she does not consider the very real possibility that women committed for trial are more likely to be acquitted than men, and if convicted, less likely to be sentenced to imprisonment.[30]

Her data on the tax problems of working women are equally distorted. This is a real problem and there is a need for an accurate statistical analysis. The case is not improved and indeed it may be damaged by the misleading or incompetent presentation of atypical cases. We are told of the heartbreaking predicament of a poor married headmistress earning £1,900 a year, of which she pays £1,010 in tax.[31] What we are not told is that to be liable for such taxation, she must have been married to a husband very much in the upper income bracket. There is no question that the English tax laws should have been altered long before they were, to allow for separate returns and to treat the headmistress far more equitably, regardless of her husband's salary. However, her plight is hardly typical of the tax problems of most working women, few of whom have husbands paying surtax. The tax law which assessed husbands and wives on the basis of their joint income was clearly unfair to working wives. However, it is significant that it was not Women's Lib but the Married Women's Association which was instrumental in getting it altered. Women's Lib protested, but it was other, less vociferous women's organizations that were responsible for bringing about the changes.

Throughout her book Germaine Greer displays a curiously naïve selectivity in her choice of statistics to support her arguments. We are told how badly women are treated by society, an argument rammed home by the fact that "there are more women who attempt suicide than men."[32] This was scarcely a good example to pick, since more men actually succeed in committing suicide. The discrepancy reflects the fact that many of the female suicide attempts were never really meant to succeed and were not the expressions of total despair that the taking of one's life implies.

When it is not relying on doubtful statistics to support its arguments, Women's Lib falls back on bogus science. Even Marshall McLuhan is brought out from obscure and well-deserved retirement to buttress its case.[33] John Stuart Mill is cited as an authority on psychology—which is roughly equivalent to quoting Aristotle on physics.[34]

Despite their claims to have been liberated from "feminine" types of thinking, the Women's Libbers display total ineptitude in handling scientific or quantitative data. It is their ineptitude in these fields, coupled with their conviction that the state of liberation involves a mastery of all conventionally male activities, which explains their sporadic irrational hostility to science. I share and understand their difficulties, but not their antipathy. With no pretensions to membership of the liberated elect, I have no reason to heap abuse on science and the scientists, statistics or the statisticians in the way Women's Lib is prone to do: "the great limitation of scientific thought";[35] a "fetish for the mathematical sciences";[36] "the dogmatism of science expresses the status quo as the ineluctable result of law";[37] statisticians are "professional cynics and death makers."[38]

The dogmatism of science is as nothing to the dogmatism of Women's Lib, and especially to the dogmatism with which they use scientific sources: "All the *best* scientific evidence today *unmistakably* tends toward the conclusion that the female possesses, biologically and inherently, a far greater capacity for sexuality than the male . . ."[39] ". . . the best medical research points to the conclusion that sexual stereotypes have no bases in biology."[40] "Sources in the field are in hopeless disagreement about the nature of sexual differences, but the *most reasonable* among them have despaired of the ambition of any definite equation between temperament and biological nature."[41]

Clearly, Women's Lib has neglected superlative argument in favor of argument by superlatives. The Libbers' arguments ooze dogmatism. In politics there are no nonpolitical occasions, and in "sexual politics" there are no "nonpolitical" facts. All facts are decided by whether or not they fit their ideological framework, and a politically free inquiry has no place in a world preempted by politics and ideology. All statements are assessed in terms of their conformity to one ideology or another. In fact, the terms "ideology" and "politics" as used by Women's Lib become entirely meaningless. The way psychologists and social scientists look at sex roles and the differences between the sexes may have a political and ideological component, but the area of overlap with activities and modes of thinking that we unequivocally term "ideology" or "politics" is limited. On a strong definition of "ideology" or "politics," our attitudes to sex roles are neither. Only by weakening these definitions to the point where they become meaningless can the view that everything is politics, that everything is ideology, be upheld. The Women's Libbers are caught on one or the other prong of an unavoidable fork: if they use strong definitions of ideology or politics, their arguments are false; if they use weak definitions, their arguments are trivial.

The Women's Lib dogmatism in argument shades over into a general authoritarianism. An official of the Israeli kibbutzim commented on Women's Lib: "In discussing the women's problem in the United States, I have often been asked: 'Why doesn't the kibbutz *draft* women into managerial jobs even if they are not inclined to accept them? Why doesn't the kibbutz draft men into early child care? . . .' "[42] The use of the term "draft" clearly indicates the methods that Women's Lib would be prepared to use to achieve the chimeric goal of liberation.

Ad hominem or *ad feminam* arguments are not sufficient in themselves to defeat Women's Lib. The bulk of the anti–Women's Lib case rests on a discussion of the issues rather than the personalities and their methods, but we cannot brush aside the fact that the Women's Lib movement is peculiarly and inextricably tied up with the individual hang-ups of its members. It advocates a universal change in the position of all women to solve the admittedly severe problems of certain small minorities—either those with eccentric sexual tastes or life styles or those who, for psychological reasons, are unable to form stable and fulfilling human relationships. Unfair attempts have been made to label the movement as nothing more than organized lesbianism; it has been very easy for Women's Lib to defeat such a mass accusation, obscuring in the process the fact that the movement does contain a large number of individual lesbians and that this must have an impact on its attitudes and policies. A number of the lesbian members of Women's Lib honestly and openly affirm their position in the movement,[43] and a number of other members are acutely and openly uncomfortable about the movement's growing obsession with this issue. Betty Friedan displays just such a concern: "We had an abortion march, or what was supposed to be an abortion march . . . Kate Millett was the first speaker, I the last. But instead of talking about abortion and child-care centres she talked about lesbianism. Women I didn't know were handing out lavender armbands and leaflets saying that since Kate had been called a lesbian, all women must show their solidarity by becoming in effect 'political lesbians'. . . I also warned that to let this movement be diverted by a sexual red herring would destroy us."[44] Betty Friedan has reason to be alarmed, for the lesbians see themselves as the vanguard of the movement: "Lesbians, because they are not afraid of being abandoned by men, are less reluctant to express hostiliy toward the male class—the oppressors of women . . . if hostility to men causes lesbianism, then it seems to me that in a male-dominated society, lesbianism is a sign of mental health."[45]

Clearly, there is a need for society to be more tolerant of homosexuals of both sexes. It is also true that if the goals of Women's Lib were achieved, both the identity and the discrimination problems experienced by the lesbian would disappear. "For lesbians Women's Liberation is not an intellectual or emotional luxury, but a personal imperative."[46] To destroy a life style accepted and valued by the vast majority of women so as to accommodate a minority sexual taste is both drastic and absurd. Women's Lib claims that the achievement of total liberation would transform the lives of all women for the better; the truth is that it would transform only the lives of women with strong lesbian tendencies. The fact that it would is a strong reproach to society, but there are simpler and milder ways of alleviating the lesbians' plight than forcing all women into an unwanted and undesirable general liberation.

Lesbians are not the only women with special problems in the Women's Lib movement. The plight of the hyperaggressive woman in our society is also an unenviable one, and many Women's Lib members and leaders come into this category: "Aggressive behaviour in women tends to be strongly disapproved of in our society. For most women this does not create any problems since they are constitutionally less aggressive than men and glad to avoid the problems that male aggression creates for the participants. For these few women, however, who even by male standards are abnormally aggressive, society provides no outlets and the social constraints on women exhibiting aggressive behaviour are especially onerous for them. They cannot state their problem directly for demands that (for instance) our society should permit the recruitment of female combat troops or encourage women to make direct physical passes at men who attract them would be met with refusal and ridicule."[47] As the emancipation of women becomes more complete, the hyperaggressive female feels even more apart from the rest of society; she no longer has the comfort of seeing her own particular grievance apparently submerged in the general, more justified grievances of all women denied their rightful opportunities. What such a woman needs is not a reforming movement that might actually succeed, but a millenarian movement of perpetual confrontations which will allow her to define her personal problems as the social problems of society, regardless of the actual state of society at the time. Whether they themselves are hyperaggressive or not, many members of Women's Lib have a curious fascination with male aggression. Germaine Greer denies such a fascination: "At various stages in my life I have lived with men of known violence, two of whom had convictions for Grievous Bodily Harm and in no case was I ever offered any physical aggression, because it was abundantly clear from my attitude that I was not impressed by it."[48] Very few men are "of known violence" and an infinitely small proportion have convictions for Grievous Bodily Harm (her capitals, not mine). The odds against her living with two such men by chance are enormous. If she is not "impressed" by "physical aggression," why did she choose such long odds?

The most important minority that flocks to join Women's Lib consists of those women who find personal relationships intensely difficult or who long for a world where human relationships involve no effort, no responsibility, and where success is guaranteed in advance. After plodding through book after book, tract after tract from Women's Lib, I was struck by the overwhelming contrast between the deep personal unhappiness that these women had known and the confidence with which they declared that human relationships, characterized by total joy and tenderness, would be painlessly achieved by all if only the stage of liberation were reached.

The whole movement has a schizoid character—the members compensate for their failure in real human relationships by creating an illusory ideal world of fondness, intimacy and delight.[49] If only, if only, they seem to cry, if only there were no husbands and wives, no parents and children, no structured relationships at all, then we would all be given unlimited and undemanding affection by all those around us. If only everything were different, how happy I would be . . . If some things were different, many people would undoubtedly be happier. But no change, however drastic, that Women's Lib has advocated, no universal panacea that they have offered, could ever do away with the problems and decisions that men and women face every day, that are intrinsic to life and relationships. Their attempt to codify the problems of personal relationships and reduce them to dead protests and glib slogans amenable to universal solutions is bound to be defeated. Liberation is an ever-shifting horizon, a total ideology that can never fulfill its promises. It acts as a temporary palliative for its true believers by generalizing their specific problems into universal grievances. It has the therapeutic quality of providing emotionally charged rituals of solidarity in hatred—it is the amphetamine of its believers.

The Female Woman

This book has one element in common with Women's Lib—it does not end in plans, projects and blueprints. Women's Lib tracts do not end on such a note because the Libbers' thinking is entirely destructive and vacuous; presumably having destroyed all institutions and relationships, they propose to hold a bonfire on the ruins. From all this destruction we are assured that "new values will emerge in response to new conditions."[1] One wonders what sort of crippled, mutant phoenix will emerge from the charred stroller tires, the burned-out pots and pans, the twisted, molten spin-dryers, around which liberated females would dance their wild corroboree.

This book is destructive for a different reason—it has sought the destruction not of a society, but of a potential threat to it. There is no need for me to set out the society of the future, since the changes and reforms will be built on the society of the present. I have had no horror stories to tell, and no death bells to ring; optimism and reform cannot be expressed as violently and as vigorously as hatred, alienation, mockery turned to loathing. I may have blown only piccolos and hardly ever trumpets for familiar institutions, but it is difficult to be extreme in favor of what exists without sinking into a bog of platitudes—a platitude is, after all, nothing but a violent endorsement of the obvious. We have custom and commitment on our side, but not easy imagery.

To trace the whole argument of the Women's Libbers is to untangle a web of badly thought out attacks on life itself. The Lib leaders have sought not merely to attack a series of specific ills which need remedy but to question and destroy the whole concept of woman. They can point to no society, no moment in the world's evolution, no clan or tribe, where what they seek to establish has even remotely been prefigured.

An apologist for Women's Lib has an impossible job on her hands: she has to establish that the liberated world can be achieved; that such a world is worth achieving; and that the cost of achieving it is not so great that we shall lose much more than we can ever hope to gain. She will have history against her. At no time has such a world existed. She will find no support in science. The evidence increasingly shows real, innate differences between men and women. And if she looks for popular acclaim, she will find that her message is incurably upper-middle-class. Above all, she has to fight the pervasive experience of people who know that the reason why women tend to look after babies more than men is that they tend to bear and suckle the babies in the first place. The apologist for Women's Lib has a hard task ahead, and without clear evidence either of divine intervention or of some shattering, world-wide genetic mutation, she is not going to get very far.

Why, then, has Women's Lib got as far as it has? Clearly, part of the reason is that women have very real grievances and can, therefore, easily feel that the movement is but an extension of the fight for women's rights. They may object to the manifestations of the extremists, but they can comfort themselves with the thought that it is all part of the emancipation battle. I have shown that it is not, and that liberation is not merely an extension of the emancipation of women. The Women's Libbers' concentration on glamorous, trivial targets has naturally attracted the publicity which they have been at such excruciating pains to seek. The strident voice is not only heard, it drowns all competing calls. The Women's Libbers do not know where they are going, but the rest of us are curious. Perhaps we can only answer this question by posing another one: Why did the movement burst into a one-thousand-candlepower flame at this particular time? There is no mystery, of course, for the true believers: it is simply a continuation of the great drive for women's emancipation that crescendoed in the early years of this century, and, by implication, the future will show that it is as reactionary and futile to oppose Women's Lib now as it is in retrospect to have opposed the demands of the early feminists. Kate Millett refers to this earlier period as the sexual revolution, first phase—and then mysteriously: ". . . reaction came; slowly, powerfully, the great impetus of the sexual revolution was brought to a halt";[2] the counterrevolution of 1930–1960 had begun. This concept of the counterrevolution is an ideological necessity for Women's Lib if the movement is to be seen as an extension of women's earlier struggles, if it is to benefit from the faint echoes of Carrie Nation's applause, if it is to be invested with the same aura of inevitability that surrounds the early feminist movements.

Liberationists talk as if women's position in that period did not just remain static but actually deteriorated, and that even the Western democracies were held tight in the grip of an antifeminist ideology; it was a period which they believed to be dominated by the theories of Sigmund Freud, who had in fact completed most of his major creative work and had gained world-wide recognition before the "counterrevolution" had even begun. Freud and his followers have the distinction of being almost the only psychologists whom the leaders of Women's Lib have bothered to read, a distinction that they probably owe to the lack of quantitative experimental data in their work; they are able to attack the whole of psychology by attacking Freud because his is the only psychology they know.

In fact, the period of counterrevolution was about the only

period in history when psychologists almost universally believed that sex differences were largely determined by environmental and cultural factors.[3] Even among the neo-Freudians there was "a shift in emphasis from the inner determinants, important in the genesis of personality to the socio-cultural or outer determinants."[4] Ironically, the counterrevolutionary period was the very period in which the monopoly of research by men and women who had an almost Women's Lib bias in favor of cultural and environmental explanations of sex differences prepared the ground for the Women's Lib movement of the 1960s. There is an even greater irony in the fact that the crass assertions of Women's Lib stimulated the detailed research that led to the overturning of the earlier theories on which the most crucial ideological assumptions of Women's Lib are based.

It is easy to show in this way that the Women's Libbers have divided history into a series of arbitrary periods for which the exactly reverse arguments can convincingly be put forward. If there is no continuity with the early feminists, then why did Women's Lib start up for the first time in the 1960s?

Women's Lib is, in fact, a movement born of an identity crisis whose activities only deepen and intensify this crisis. In the 1960s the thinking public became more acutely aware of the dangers of overpopulation. With slogans like "Come Back, Malthus—All Is Forgiven" and "Babies Are Pollution," society's attitude to what had historically been woman's primary role could hardly remain the same—the maternal role was devalued, and this had spillover effects for all aspects of femaleness.[5] Identity crises have an unfortunate propensity for deepening themselves: doubt sets off counter-doubt, which triggers off yet more lack of confidence in all the female roles. But doubt does not resonate forever, especially as the initial impact of the population scare is over. The birth rate is falling toward a replacement level in countries as diverse as Sweden, Japan, Britain and America; in most of these countries, governments have now adopted family-planning measures, and the overpopulation fear will soon be over for the industrial nations of the West—a development that will greatly help to restore the status of the maternal role. Women will regain their self-confident femaleness and Women's Lib will fall on even deafer ears.[6]

The only social change that coincides with both the culmination of the feminist movement and the growth of Women's Lib is the rate of growth of sexual permissiveness, which was rapid in the 1920s and the 1960s, and relatively slow in between.[7] Now that greater freedom in sexual relationships has become so widely accepted, it is difficult to see how any further great growth could occur either to sustain Women's Lib or as a result of Women's Lib activities.

Far from time being on its side, Women's Lib is a product of specifically temporary circumstances, and as the social conditions that gave birth to this movement recede in time and importance, so Women's Lib will decline. Also, like all transient but spectacular phenomena, Women's Lib has received an inordinate amount of publicity from the media, and like all such overexposed movements, it will soon become a bore. So far, the Women's Liberation movement has enjoyed the great advantage of being an unpopular movement whose unpopularity is never clearly stated; the time has now come for this unpopularity to be made articulate and vociferous. The real grievances upon which Women's Lib trades, and its false, proud, proprietorial attitude to all antidiscrimination reforms, have made it seem almost feudal to stand out against the movement. Most people have sensed the narrow base of Women's Lib and detected its false rationale and faulty reasoning. Yet many women have avoided outright attack for fear of being dubbed reactionary or of giving ammunition to those who would hold up the very necessary measures of emancipation which this book supports.

I have sought to show that both common and uncommon sense demands emancipation but denies the tenets of Women's Lib. We are different from men—different but equal. The roles which we can play in society are not artificially restricted by some eternal international conspiracy in which all men since the Stone Age have joined. There is no Paleolithic plot to hold us back. The female woman will assert her right to be free, but she will refuse to allow the Libbers to force her to become an ersatz man. The frenetic extremism of Women's Lib seeks not to emancipate women, but to destroy society. The hand that refuses to rock the cradle is all too eager to overturn the world. The female woman wants to live as an equal in the world, not to destroy it in the vain search for an instant millennium. Her search for emancipation will improve and reform; Women's Liberation will deface and destroy.

I hope that *The Female Woman* will help to crystallize the unpopularity of Women's Lib and will encourage all those women who have been sneered at by Women's Lib for far too long to hit back—to hit back with the strength and confidence of being female women.

Notes

Full publication details of books, journals and articles will be found in the Bibliography.

THE EMANCIPATED WOMAN

1. M. C. Bradbrook, *That Infidel Place.*
2. Christie Davies, *Permissive Britain,* Chapter 4.
3. I deliberately use the term "femaleness" rather than "feminity" because words like "feminine," "femininity," have been debased out of existence by the attacks of Women's Libbers—they have not won a victory but they have captured a word.
4. Germaine Greer, *The Female Eunuch,* p. 65.
5. *Ibid.,* p. 85.
6. Kate Millett, *Sexual Politics,* pp. 186–87.
7. *Ibid.,* p. 26.
8. Greer, p. 282.
9. *Ibid.,* pp. 150–52; Millett, p. 231.
10. Davies, *op. cit.,* Chapter 4.
11. Erwin Stengel, *Suicide and Attempted Suicide,* p. 21.
12. Millett, pp. 36, 56, 103, 119, 121; Greer, p. 75; Shulamith Firestone, *The Dialectic of Sex,* pp. 103 ff.; Juliet Mitchell, *Woman's Estate,* pp. 14–15.
13. D. M. Potts, "Which Is the Weaker Sex?," *Journal of Biosocial Science.* *See* Harrison and Peel.
14. *The Times,* of London, December 12, 1972.

15. Potts, *op. cit.*
16. Millett, p. 37.
17. They may do so for one day a year in curious folk festivals—but no more than that.

THE NATURAL WOMAN

1. Millett, *Sexual Politics*, p. 27, footnote 7.
2. *Ibid.*, p. 93.
3. Greer, *The Female Eunuch*, p. 29.
4. Corinne Hutt, *Males and Females*, p. 17.
5. John Stuart Mill, *The Subjection of Women*, p. 451.
6. *Ibid.*
7. Greer, pp. 26–27.
8. Millett, p. 27 and pp. 28–29 (my italics).
9. George Orwell, *1984*, pp. 44–75. Newspeak seems the ideal language for liberated women!
10. Corinne Hutt, "Neuroendocrinological, Behavioural, and Intellectual Aspects of Sexual Differentiation in Human Development," in C. Ormsted and D. C. Taylor, *Gender Differences: Their Ontogeny and Significance*, p. 73.
11. Hutt, *Males and Females*, p. 70.
12. A. A. Ehrhardt, R. Epstein and J. Money, "Foetal Androgens and Female Gender Identity in the Early Treated Andrenogenital Syndrome," *Johns Hopkins Medical Journal*, Vol. 122 (1968), pp. 160 ff.
13. C. H. Phoenix, R. W. Goy, A. A. Gerall and W. C. Young, "Organising Action of Prenatally Administered Testosterone Propionate on the Tissues Mediating Mating Behaviour in the Female Guinea Pig," *Endocrinology* 65 (1969), pp. 369–82.
14. Hutt, *Males and Females*, p. 25; P. E. Polari, "Sex Chromosome Anomalies," in Ormsted and Taylor, *op. cit.*, pp. 29–30.
15. John Money, "Sexual Dimorphism and Homosexual Gender Identity," *Psychological Bulletin*, Vol. 74 (1970), pp. 425–40.
16. Hutt, *Males and Females*, p. 73; *see also* Money, *op. cit.*
17. A. Heim, *Intelligence and Personality*, pp. 136–45; or D. C. Taylor and C. Ormsted, "Ontogenic Analysis of Sex Ratios in Disease," in Ormsted and Taylor, *op. cit.*, pp. 232–33.
18. Margaret Ormsted, "Gender and Intrauterine Growth," in Ormsted and Taylor, *op. cit.*, p. 187.
19. Taylor and Ormsted in Ormsted and Taylor, *op. cit.*, p. 232.
20. G. W. Harris, "Sex Hormones, Brain Development and Brain Function," the Upjohn Lecture of the Endocrine Society, *Endocrinology*, Vol. 75 (1964), pp. 627–48.
21. Firestone, *The Dialectic of Sex*, p. 221.

22. Greer, p. 15.
23. Taylor and Ormsted in Ormsted and Taylor, *op. cit.*, p. 224.
24. Hutt, *Males and Females*, pp. 94–95.
25. Anthony W. H. Buffery and Jeffrey A. Gray, "Sex Differences in the Development of Spatial and Linguistic Skills," in Ormsted and Taylor, *op. cit.*, p. 123.
26. *Ibid.*, p. 125.
27. Hutt, *Males and Females*, p. 92.
28. Buffery and Gray, in Ormsted and Taylor, *op. cit.*, p. 129.
29. J. L. M. Dawson, "Cultural and Physiological Influences upon Spatial-Perceptual Processes in West Africa," *International Journal of Psychology*, Vol. 2 (1967), pp. 115–28 and pp. 171–85 (2 parts).
30. Greer, p. 99.
31. Buffery and Gray, in Ormsted and Taylor, *op. cit.*, p. 147.
32. R. J. Andrews and L. J. Rogers, "Testosterone—Effects on Search Behaviour and Persistence," *Nature*, Vol. 237, No. 5354 (June 9, 1972).
33. E. L. Klaiber, D. M. Broverman and Y. Kobayashi, "The Automatization Cognitive Style, Androgens and Monoamine Oxidase," *Psychopharmacologia*, Vol. II (1967).
34. *Ibid.* (my italics).
35. It would have no effect on them after they have left the womb; cf. Andrews and Rogers, *op. cit.*
36. Hutt, *Males and Females*, pp. 103–4 and p. 119.
37. Greer, p. 29.
38. Money, *op. cit.*; Money, "The Influence of Hormones on Sexual Behaviour," *Annual Review of Medicine*, Vol. 16 (1965); Ehrhardt et al., *op. cit.*; Hutt, "Neuroendocrinological . . . Aspects of Sexual Differentiation . . ." in Ormsted and Taylor, *op cit.*, p. 78.
39. Millett, pp. 31–32.
40. Clifford J. Jolly, "The Seed-Eaters: A New Model of Hominid Differentiation Based on a Baboon Analogy," *Man* (1970), pp. 5 ff.
41. Hutt, in Ormsted and Taylor, *op. cit.*, p. 91.
42. *Ibid.*, p. 85.
43. Hutt, *Males and Females*, pp. 54–55 (my italics).
44. M. Spiro, *Children of the Kibbutz*, pp. 247–48.
45. *Ibid.*, p. 83.
46. *Ibid.*, p. 84.
47. David Cooper, *The Death of the Family*, p. 107.

THE SEXUAL WOMAN

1. *The Guardian*, January 3, 1972.
2. This is a typical ideal Women's Lib argument.

3. S. Andreski, *Parasitism and Subversion*, pp. 47 ff.
4. M. Dennis, F. M. Henriques and D. Slaughter, *Coal Is Our Life*, pp. 228 ff.
5. G. L. Gingsberg, A. Williams, W. A. Frosch and T. Schapiro, "The New Impotence," *Archives General Psychiatry*, Vol. 26 (1972). *See also* M. Puxon and S. Dawkins, "Non Consummation of Marriage," *Medicine, Science and the Law*, Vol. 4 (1964), p. 15.
6. Millett, *Sexual Politics*, pp. 146, 253, 279, 285–93; 14, 316; 44, 45–46, 50, 195–96; 184, 335; 50, 62, 99 ff., 217, 220, 363; 238, 282, 297–313, 314–35, 336 ff., 352 ff., and many others.
7. Lord Devlin, *The Enforcement of Morals*, p. 6.
8. Greer, quoted in *The Female Eunuch*, pp. 257–58.
9. *Ibid.*, p. 257.
10. Hubert Selby, *Last Exit to Brooklyn*, p. 111.
11. London *Daily Telegraph*, November 2, 1972.
12. Greer, p. 257.
13. Thomas Hobbes, *Leviathan*, p. 100.
14. Millett, pp. 17–18.
15. E. M. Schur, *Crimes without Victims*.
16. Samuel Igra, *Germany's National Vice*, p. 101.
17. Jerry Allen, *The Sea Years of Joseph Conrad*, p. 280, is a good instance of this.
18. Malinowski writes about the Trobriand Islanders who told him that rape by women was common in their community, but he never actually observed this, and he refused to believe it. B. Malinowski, *The Sexual Life of Savages*.
19. Greer, p. 42.
20. *Loc. cit.*
21. Anthony Storr, *Human Aggression*, pp. 91–92.
22. Quoted in Millett, p. 252. *See also* D. H. Lawrence, *Lady Chatterley's Lover*, in which a miner's widow tells Lady Chatterley of her husband's loss of his sexual eagerness after he had seen her undergo a particularly painful childbirth.
23. Quoted in Millett, p. 252, from D. H. Lawrence, *Sons and Lovers*, p. 279.
24. Greer, p. 92.
25. Millett, p. 206.
26. Quoted in Millett, p. 206, from Marie N. Robinson, *The Power of Sexual Surrender* (New York, Doubleday, 1959), p. 158.
27. Quoted in Millett, p. 206, from Helene Deutsch, *The Psychology of Women*, II (New York, Grune & Stratton, 1945), p. 103.
28. Germaine Greer, "Seduction Is a Four Letter Word," *Playboy* (January 1973), p. 228.
29. "J," *The Sensuous Woman*, back cover.

30. *Ibid.*, pp. 94–95.
31. *Ibid.*, p. 58.
32. *Ibid.*, p. 79.
33. Corinne Hutt, *Males and Females*, p. 84: "Watson simply wanted to condition the babies to 'look at' a spot of light whenever it appeared. The remarkable fact was that he was only able to do so successfully if he used sounds as reinforcements for the girls and lights as reinforcements for the boys."
34. Cf. Money, "Sexual Dimorphism and Homosexual Gender Identity," *Psychological Bulletin*, Vol. 74 (1970), pp. 425–40.
35. John Money, "The Influence of Hormones on Sexual Behaviour," *Annual Review of Medicine*, Vol. 16 (1965).
36. B. Kutchinsky, *Studies on Pornography and Sex Crimes in Denmark.*
37. *The Wolfenden Report*, para. 223: "The great majority of prostitutes are women whose psychological make-up is such that they choose this life because they find in it a style of living which is easier, freer and more profitable than would be provided by any other occupation."
38. Millett, p. 123, footnote 145.
39. M. Schofield, *The Sexual Behaviour of Young People.*
40. Millett, pp. 117–18.
41. This can be seen from a comparison of data in the two Kinsey reports. See A. Kinsey et al., *Sexual Behaviour in the Human Male*, 1949; *Sexual Behaviour in the Human Female*, 1953.
42. Martha Shelley, "Notes of a Radical Lesbian," in *Sisterhood is Powerful*, ed. Robin Morgan, pp. 306–11; *see also* Greer, p. 293.
43. Quoted in Simone de Beauvoir, *The Second Sex*, p. 359.
44. *Loc. cit.*
45. Greer, p. 58.
46. *Ibid.*, p. 60.
47. *Ibid.*, p. 94.
48. Harris Opinion Poll, London *Daily Express* (April 20, 1972).
49. E. Durkheim, *The Division of Labour in Society*, p. 406.
50. D. Riesman, N. Glazer and R. Denny, *The Lonely Crowd.*
51. Greer, p. 294.
52. *Ibid.*, p. 173.
53. Cooper, *The Death of the Family*, p. 123.
54. *Ibid.*, p. 41.
55. Greer, p. 180.
56. *Loc. cit.*
57. *Loc. cit.*
58. *Loc. cit.*
59. *Ibid.*, p. 18.

THE FAMILY WOMAN

1. Eva Figes, *Patriarchal Attitudes*, p. 194.
2. Millett, *Sexual Politics*, pp. 126–27.
3. Firestone, *The Dialectic of Sex*, p. 222.
4. Greer, *The Female Eunuch*, pp. 288–89. There are many other references to her parents' unhappy marriage, and even a reference to the unhappy marriage of her "fairy" godparents creeps into the dedication on p. 5.
5. *The Montreal Gazette*, May 27, 1972.
6. De Beauvoir, *The Second Sex*, p. 119.
7. Plato, *The Symposium*, p. 64.
8. Edward Carpenter, *Love's Coming of Age*, pp. 149–50.
9. Nemone Lethbridge, "Man on the Moon," in *Woman on Woman*, ed. Margaret Laing, pp. 87–88.
10. Millett, p. 126.
11. Firestone, *op. cit.*, pp. 188–89.
12. *Ibid.*, p. 217.
13. Discussion in Millett, pp. 224–25.
14. *Ibid.*, p. 126.
15. Jaroslav Hasek, *The Good Soldier Schweik*, p. 33.
16. Firestone, *op. cit.*, p. 215.
17. M. Young and P. Wilmott, *Family and Kinship in East London* and *Family and Class in a London Suburb;* E. Litwak, "The Extended Family and Occupational Mobility" and "The Extended Family and Geographical Mobility," *American Sociological Review* (February and June 1960).
18. Millett, pp. 126–27.
19. Firestone, op. cit., p. 215.
20. Greer, p. 235.
21. Firestone, *op. cit.*, p. 224.
22. "But principally I hate and detest that animal called man; although I heartily love John, Peter, Thomas and so forth." Jonathan Swift in a letter to Pope, September 29, 1725.
23. Greer, p. 22.
24. Greer in a debate at the Cambridge Union Society against William F. Buckley Jr., Michaelmas 1972.
25. Milton Rokeach, *The Open and Closed Mind*, pp. 51–53.
26. Firestone, *op. cit.*, p. 222.
27. Millett, p. 62.
28. Cooper, *The Death of the Family*, p. 17.
29. *Ibid.*, p. 10.

30. Firestone, *op. cit.*, p. 217.
31. Max Weber, *The Protestant Ethic and the Spirit of Capitalism*, pp. 181–82.
32. Greer, p. 221.
33. *Ibid.*, p. 235.
34. *Ibid.*, p. 236.
35. Luigi Pirandello, "The Cooper's Cockerels," in *Pirandello's Short Stories*, p. 10.
36. Descriptions of the southern Italian spider cults in I. Lewis, *Ecstatic Religion.*
37. Millett, p. 158 (see in text and in footnote 2).
38. *Ibid.*, p. 171.
39. *Ibid.*, p. 173.
40. Greer, p. 300.
41. *Ibid.*, p. 301.
42. Igra, *Germany's National Vice*, p. 87.
43. *Ibid.*, p. 91.
44. *Ibid.*, p. 90.
45. Hans Blüher, *Rolle der Erotik in der männlichen Gesellschaft*, Vol. 2, p. 91.
46. Igra, *op. cit.*, p. 90.
47. Alfred Baumler, *Mannerbund und Wissenschaft*, p. 86.
48. Igra, *op. cit.*, p. 98.
49. *Ibid.*, p. 99.
50. Menachem Gerson, "Women in the Kibbutz," *American Journal of Orthopsychiatry*, Vol. 41, No. 4 (July 1971).
51. *Ibid.*
52. *Ibid.*
53. *Newsweek* (October 23, 1972).
54. Bruno Bettelheim, *The Children of the Dream*, p. 165.
55. *Ibid.*, p. 127.
56. *Ibid.*, p. 107.
57. *Ibid.*, p. 95.
58. *Ibid.*, p. 244.
59. *Newsweek* (October 23, 1972).
60. Bettelheim, *op. cit.*, p. 252.
61. Antony Clare, "R. D. Laing Returns to the Fold," *The Spectator* (February 3, 1973).
62. Quoted in Susan Jacoby, *The Friendship Barrier*. See also *The Sunday Times*, August 20, 1972.
63. *The Sunday Times*, October 15, 1972.
64. Helena Znaniecki Lopata, *Occupation Housewife*, p. 76.
65. *Ibid.*, p. 639.
66. *Ibid.*, p. 373.

THE WORKING WOMAN

1. Millett, *Sexual Politics*, p. 26.
2. David Magarshack's "Foreword" to his translation of Tolstoy's *Anna Karenina*, pp. x–xiv.
3. T. S. Eliot, *The Confidential Clerk*, p. 41.
4. *The Sunday Times*, February 11, 1973.
5. Georges Simenon, *The Door*, pp. 68–69.
6. H. G. Wells, *The History of Mr Polly*, p. 54.
7. Michael Fogarty, Rhona Rapoport and Robert Rapoport, *Women in Top Jobs: The Next Move.*
8. Ministry of Labour *Gazette*, throughout the 1960s.
9. B. T. Davies, "Comparative Employability of Men and Women in Different Industries," *Journal of Biosocial Science. See* Harrison and Peel.
10. Quoted in Lopata, *Occupation Housewife*, p. 142, footnote 4.
11. Perhaps we could satisfy them by defining divorce as breach of contract, alimony as a redundancy payment, and by holding golden-wedding celebrations in the factory canteen.
12. Greer, *The Female Eunuch*, p. 279.
13. *Ibid.,* pp. 289 and 282.
14. H. F. Harlow, "The Nature of Love," *American Psychologist*, 13 (1958), pp. 673–85; H. F. Harlow and R. R. Zimmerman, "Affectional Responses in the Infant Monkey," *Science*, 130 (1959), pp. 421–32.
15. John Bowlby, *Child Care and the Growth of Love* and *Attachment and Loss.*
16. Robert Jay Lifton, *Revolutionary Immortality.*
17. De Beauvoir, *The Second Sex*, p. 634.
18. Lopata, *op. cit.,* p. 204.
19. B. T. Davies, *op. cit.*
20. Germaine Greer, *The Sunday Times*, February 13, 1972.
21. *Ibid.*
22. B. T. Davies, *op. cit.*
23. *Ibid.*
24. Corinne Hutt, *Males and Females*, p. 97.
25. H. Fairweather and S. J. Hutt, "Sex Differences in a Perceptual-motor Skill in Children," in Ormsted and Taylor, *Gender Differences*, p. 171.
26. Corinne Hutt, p. 97.
27. Based on data in Ormsted and Taylor, *op. cit.,* pp. 106, 113, 126, 132; and Corinne Hutt, pp. 87, 92, 96.

28. Corinne Hutt, pp. 87–96.
29. Michael Fogarty, A. J. Allen, Isobel Allen and Patricia Walters, *Women in Top Jobs*, p. 134.
30. Gerson, "Women in the Kibbutz."
31. Alexander Solzhenitsyn, *The First Circle*, p. 289.
32. Millett, p. 158.

THE MALE MAN

1. Greer, *The Female Eunuch*, p. 331.
2. *Ibid.*, p. 133.
3. Corinne Hutt, *Males and Females*, p. 23.
4. Taylor and Ormsted, "The Nature of Gender Differences Explored Through Ontogenic Analyses of Sex Ratios in Disease," in Ormsted and Taylor, *Gender Differences*, p. 225.
5. *Ibid.*, p. 224.
6. Greer, p. 64.
7. Potts, "Which Is the Weaker Sex?"
8. D. B. Lynn, in *Psychological Review*, Vol. 66 (1959), p. 126.
9. Millett, *Sexual Politics*, p. 26.
10. Lynn, *op. cit.*
11. Greer, p. 78.
12. *Loc. cit.*
13. Christie Davies, *Permissive Britain*, Chapter 5.
14. Quoted in Millett, p. 103, from John Stuart Mill, *The Subjection of Women*, p. 523.
15. James Fitzjames Stephen, *Liberty, Equality and Fraternity*, Editor's Introduction by R. J. White, p. 7.
16. *Ibid.*, p. 3.
17. John Bancroft, "The Relationships between Gender Identity and Sexual Behaviour: Some Clinical Aspects," in Ormsted and Taylor, *op. cit.*, p. 64.
18. Greer, pp. 264–66.
19. Menna Gallie, "For God's Sake, Hold Your Tongue, and Let Me Love," *Cambridge Review* (November 13, 1970).
20. Millett, p. 57.
21. Lynn, *op. cit.*
22. Behavior is a better guide to reality than questionnaires, which are subject to unpredictable observer bias.
23. Ivan N. Mersh, "Personal and Social Influences in the Development of Gender Identity," in Ormsted and Taylor, *op. cit.*, p. 43.
24. Bancroft, *op. cit.*, p. 59.
25. "M," *The Sensuous Man*, pp. 23–24.

26. Joan Malleson, *Any Wife or Any Husband*, p. 90.
27. Greer, p. 47.
28. Millett, p. 327.
29. *Ibid.*, p. 47.
30. *Ibid.*, p. 209. This quote contains her own quotation from F. Lundberg and M. Farnham, *Modern Woman: The Lost Sex* (New York, Grosset and Dunlap, 1947), p. 241.
31. A. Storr, *Human Aggression*, pp. 89–90.
32. Gingsberg, Williams, Frosch and Schapiro, "The New Impotence."
33. Greer, p. 88.
34. Lionel Tiger, *Men in Groups*, pp. 80–81.
35. Greer, *The Sunday Times*, February 13, 1972.
36. B. T. Davies, "Comparative Employability of Men and Women in Different Industries."
37. G. H. Perris, *Germany and The German Emperor*, p. 65.
38. Millett, p. 104.
39. Orwell, *Inside the Whale*, pp. 46–47.
40. R. C. Sherriff, *Journey's End.*
41. The *Birkenhead* sank off South Africa on June 28, 1851. Nearly four hundred soldiers lost their lives, but not a single woman.
42. Christie Davies, *op. cit.*
43. Millett, p. 50.
44. *Ibid.*, pp. 159–68.
45. "Dexter," *Will You Be Left?*, pp. 15–29.
46. Troy Duster, *The Legislation of Morality*, Chapter 1; or J. Young, *The Drug Takers*, pp. 124–26 and p. 146.
47. Frances Heidersohn, "Sex, Crime and Society," in Harrison and Peel, *Biosocial Aspects of Sex.*
48. Kinsey et al., *Sexual Behaviour in The Human Female*, p. 121.
49. B. Kutchinsky, *Studies on Pornography and Sex Crimes in Denmark;* for a discussion of exhibitionism and peeping.
50. Tony Parker, *The Twisting Lane: Some Sex Offenders*, especially pp. 165–90.
51. Lord Devlin, *The Enforcement of Morals*, p. 12.
52. Taylor and Ormsted in Ormsted and Taylor, *op. cit.*, pp. 232–33.
53. Heidersohn, *op. cit.*
54. In 1965 in the United Kingdom there were 30,000 homeless men and only 2,000 homeless women; 29,650 men and only 2,030 women in reception centers and common lodging houses; 920 men sleeping rough and only 65 women.
55. *Newsweek* (October 23, 1972).

THE LIBERATED WOMAN?. . .
AND HER LIBERATORS

1. Greer, *The Female Eunuch,* p. 300.
2. Morgan (ed.), *Sisterhood is Powerful,* p. xxxvi.
3. Greer, p. 301.
4. B.B.C. TV, December 1972.
5. Robert Michels, *Political Parties, 1915.*
6. Greer, p. 310.
7. Valerie Solanas, *S.C.U.M. Manifesto,* p. 43.
8. *Ibid.,* p. 50. But for a sympathetic mention, see Greer, p. 308.
9. Shelley, "Notes on a Radical Lesbian."
10. *Ibid.,* pp. 308–9.
11. Millett, *Sexual Politics,* p. 55, footnote 71.
12. *Ibid.,* pp. 229, 231.
13. *Ibid.,* pp. 231–33.
14. Greer, p. 171.
15. Millett, p. 95, footnote 53.
16. See also Germaine Greer's chapter entitled "Bones," in *The Female Eunuch,* p. 30 ff.
17. Sigmund Freud, *Civilisation and Its Discontents.*
18. Millett, p. 93.
19. Greer, p. 29 (my italics).
20. With apologies to William Shakespeare. See *The Merchant of Venice,* Act 3, Scene I, Shylock speaking. Women do not need to remind men of their common humanity as the Jews needed to remind the Roman Catholic Venetians.
21. C. Ormsted and D. C. Taylor, "The Y-chromosome Message: A Point of View," in Ormsted and Taylor, *Gender Differences,* p. 245.
22. Corinne Hutt, *Males and Females,* p. 19.
23. Greer, p. 29.
24. Millett, p. 43. On Calabria *see* Greer, p. 221.
25. Dennis et al., *Coal Is Our Life;* pp. 288 ff.
26. Gingsberg et al., "The New Impotence."
27. Millett, p. 42.
28. *Ibid.,* pp. 365–77.
29. Greer, *The Sunday Times,* November 5, 1972.
30. Heidersohn, "Sex, Crime and Society," or Ann Oakley, *Sex Gender and Society.*
31. Greer, p. 122.
32. *Ibid.,* p. 281.
33. *Ibid.,* pp. 108, 144.

34. Millett, p. 95.
35. Greer, p. 107; cf. also pp. 109, 113.
36. Millett, p. 220; cf. also p. 178.
37. Greer, p. 14; cf. also p. 90.
38. *Ibid.,* p. 144.
39. Millett, p. 116 (my italics).
40. *Ibid.,* pp. 26–27, footnote 7 (my italics).
41. *Ibid.,* pp. 28–29 (my italics).
42. Gerson, "Women in the Kibbutz" (my italics).
43. Shelley in Morgan, *op. cit.,* and see also articles describing the position of lesbians in the Women's Lib movement, such as: Nanette Rainone, Martha Shelley, Lois Hart, "Lesbians Are Sisters," in *Voices from Women's Liberation,* edited by Leslie B. Tanner, p. 349; also Gene Damon, "The Least of These: The Minority Whose Screams Haven't Yet Been Heard," in Morgan, *op. cit.,* p. 297.
44. Friedan, *Vanity Fair* (October 1971), p. 71.
45. Shelley, in Morgan, *op. cit.,* p. 308.
46. Sidney Abbot and Barbara Soal, *Sappho Was a Right-On Woman: A Liberated View of Lesbianism.*
47. Christie Davies, *Permissive Britain,* Chapter 4.
48. Greer, p. 316.
49. Storr, *Human Aggression,* pp. 121–22.

THE FEMALE WOMAN

1. Greer, *The Sunday Times,* February 27, 1972.
2. Millett, *Sexual Politics,* p. 156.
3. Hutt, "Neuroendocrinological . . . Aspects . . .," in Ormsted and Taylor, *Gender Differences,* pp. 73, 106; and Hutt, *Males and Females,* pp. 69–70.
4. Thomas Colley, "The Nature and Origins of Psychological Sexual Identity," *Psychological Review,* Vol. 66, No. 3 (1959).
5. Christie Davies, *Permissive Britain,* Chapter 4.
6. The case is very different in underdeveloped countries with low growth rates and high birth rates, but Women's Lib is a phenomenon of industrial societies.
7. Christie Davies, *op. cit.,* Chapter 1.

Bibliography

ABBOT, SIDNEY, and SOAL, BARBARA, *Sappho Was a Right-On Woman: A Liberated View of Lesbianism.* New York, Stein & Day, 1970.

ALLEN, ISOBEL, *see* Fogarty, M.

ALLEN, JERRY, *The Sea Years of Joseph Conrad.* London, Methuen, 1967.

ANDREWS, R. J., and ROGERS, L. J., "Testosterone—Effects on Search Behaviour and Persistence." *Nature,* Vol. 237, No. 5354 (June 9, 1972).

ANDRESKI, S., *Parasitism and Subversion: The Case of Latin America.* London, Weidenfeld & Nicolson, 1966.

BANCROFT, JOHN, "The Relationships between Gender Identity and Sexual Behaviour: Some Clinical Aspects," in Ormsted and Taylor.

BAR-YOSEF, DR. RIKVA, "Women's Lib Is Foolishness." *Newsweek* (October 23, 1972).

BEAUVOIR, SIMONE DE, *The Second Sex.* London, Penguin, 1972.

BETTELHEIM, BRUNO, *The Children of the Dream.* London, Paladin, 1971.

BOWLBY, JOHN, *Child Care and the Growth of Love.* London, Pelican, 1953.

———, *Attachment and Loss.* 2 vols. London, Pelican, 1971.

BRADBROOK, M. C., *That Infidel Place: A Short History of Girton College, 1896–1969.* London, Chatto & Windus, 1969.

BROVERMAN, D. M., *see* Klaiber, E. L.

BUFFERY, ANTHONY, and GRAY, JEFFREY A., "Sex Differences in the Development of Spatial and Linguistic Skills," in Ormsted and Taylor.

CARPENTER, EDWARD, *Love's Coming of Age.* New York, Boni & Liveright, 1911.

CLARE, ANTONY, "R. D. Laing Returns to the Fold." *Spectator* (February 3, 1973).

COLLEY, THOMAS, "The Nature and Origins of Psychological Sexual Identity." *Psychological Review*, Vol. 66, No. 3 (1959).

COOPER, DAVID, *The Death of the Family*. London, Pelican, 1972.

DAMON, GENE, "The Least of These: The Minority Whose Screams Haven't Yet Been Heard," in Morgan, Robin.

DAVIES, B. T., "Comparative Employability of Men and Women in Different Industries." *Journal of Biosocial Science. See* Harrison, G. A., and Peel, J.

DAVIES, CHRISTIE, *Permissive Britain: Social Change in the Sixties and Seventies*. London, Pitman, 1973.

DAWKINS, S., *see* Puxon, M.

DAWSON, J. L. M., "Cultural and Physiological Influences upon Spatial-Perceptual Processes in West Africa." *International Journal of Psychology*, Vol. 2 (1967).

DE BEAUVOIR, *see* Beauvoir, Simone de.

DENNIS, M., HENRIQUES, F. M., and SLAUGHTER, D., *Coal Is Our Life*. London, Eyre & Spottiswoode, 1956.

DENNY, R., *see* Riesman, D.

DEVLIN, LORD, *The Enforcement of Morals*. London, Oxford University Press, 1965.

"DEXTER," *Will You Be Left?* London, Hutchinson, 1945.

DURKHEIM, E., *The Division of Labour in Society*. New York, Free Press, 1964.

DUSTER, TROY, *The Legislation of Morality*. New York, Free Press, 1970.

ELIOT, T. S., *The Confidential Clerk*. London, Faber, 1954.

EPSTEIN, R., *see* Ehrhardt, A. A.

EHRHARDT, A. A., EPSTEIN, R., and MONEY, J., "Foetal Androgens and Female Gender Identity in the Early Treated Andrenogenital Syndrome." *John Hopkins Medical Journal*, Vol. 122 (1968).

FAIRWEATHER, H., and HUTT, S. J., "Sex Differences in a Perceptual-motor Skill in Children," in Ormsted and Taylor.

FIGES, EVA, *Patriarchal Attitudes*. London, Panther, 1972; Faber, 1970.

FIRESTONE, SHULAMITH, *The Dialectic of Sex: The Case for Feminist Revolution*. Paladin, 1972; Cape, 1971.

FOGARTY, MICHAEL, ALLEN, ISOBEL, ALLEN, A. J., and WALTER, PATRICIA, *Women in Top Jobs*. London, Allen & Unwin, 1971.

FOGARTY, MICHAEL, RAPOPORT, RHONA, and RAPOPORT, ROBERT, *Women in Top Jobs: The Next Move*, P.E.P. [Political and Economic Planning] Broadsheet No. 535 (1971).

FREUD, S., *Civilisation and Its Discontents* (1930), London, Hogarth, 1963.

FRIEDAN, BETTY, in *Vanity Fair* (October 1971).

FROSCH, *see* Gingsberg, G. L.

GALLIE, MENNA, "For God's Sake, Hold Your Tongue, and Let Me Love." *Cambridge Review* (November 13, 1970).

GERALL, A. A., *see* Phoenix, C. H.

GERSON, MENACHEM, "Women in the Kibbutz." *American Journal of Orthopsychiatry*, Vol. 41, No. 4 (July 1971).

GINGSBERG, G. L., WILLIAMS, A., FROSCH, W. A., and SCHAPIRO, T., "The New Impotence." *Archives General Psychiatry*, Vol. 26 (1972).

GLAZER, N., *see* Riesman, D.

GOY, R. W., *see* Phoenix, C. H.

GRAY, JEFFRY A., *see* Buffery, Anthony W. H.

GREER, GERMAINE, *The Female Eunuch.* London, MacGibbon & Kee, 1970.

———, articles in *The Sunday Times* of London (February 13 and 27, and November 5, 1972).

———, "Seduction Is a Four Letter Word," *Playboy* (January 1973).

HARLOW, H. F., "The Nature of Love." *American Psychologist*, 13 (1958).

———, and ZIMMERMAN, R. R., "Affectional Responses in the Infant Monkey." *Science*, 130 (1959).

HARRIS, G. W., "Sex Hormones, Brain Development and Brain Function." The Upjohn Lecture of the Endocrine Society. *Endocrinology*, Vol. 75 (1964).

HARRISON, G. A., and PEEL, J. (eds.), *Biosocial Aspects of Sex.* Proceedings of the 6th Annual Symposium of the Eugenics Society, Supplement No. 2 to the *Journal of Biosocial Science* (May 1970).

HASEK, JAROSLAV, *The Good Soldier Schweik.* London, Penguin, 1968.

HEIDERSOHN, FRANCES, "Sex, Crime and Society," in Harrison and Peel.

HEIM, A., *Intelligence and Personality.* London, Pelican, 1970.

HENRIQUES, F. M., *see* Dennis, M.

HOBBES, THOMAS, *Leviathan.* New York, Collier Books, 1962.

HUTT, CORINNE, *Males and Females.* London, Penguin, 1972.

———, "Neuroendocrinological, Behavioural and Intellectual Aspects of Sexual Differentiation in Human Development," in Ormsted and Taylor.

HUTT, S. J., *see* Fairweather, H.

IGRA, SAMUEL, *Germany's National Vice.* London, Quality Press, 1945.

"J," *The Sensuous Woman.* London, Mayflower Books (Granada), 1971.

JACOBY, SUSAN, *The Friendship Barrier.* London, Bodley Head, 1972.

JOLLY, CLIFFORD J., "The Seed-Eaters: A New Model of Hominid Differentiation Based on a Baboon Analogy." *Man*, the Journal of the Royal Anthropological Institute, new series, Vol. 5 (1970).

KINSEY, A., et al., *Sexual Behaviour in the Human Male.* Saunders, Philadelphia, 1949.

———, *Sexual Behaviour in the Human Female.* Philadelphia, Saunders, 1953.

KLAIBER, E. L., BROVERMAN, D. M., and KOBAYASHI, Y., "The Automization Cognitive Style, Androgens and Monoamine Oxidase." *Psychopharmacologia*, Vol. II (1967).

KOBAYASHI, Y., *see* Klaiber, E. L.

KUTCHINSKY, B., *Studies on Pornography and Sex Crimes in Denmark.* New Social Science Monographs, November 1970.

LAWRENCE, D. H., *Lady Chatterley's Lover.* London, Heinemann, 1960.

LETHBRIDGE, NEMONE, "Man on the Moon," in *Woman on Woman,* edited by Margaret Laing. London, Sidgwick & Jackson, 1971.

LEWIS, I., *Ecstatic Religion. An Anthropological Study of Shamanism and Spirit Possession.* London, Penguin, 1972.

LIFTON, ROBERT JAY, *Revolutionary Immortality.* London, Penguin, 1970.

LITWAK, E., "The Extended Family and Occupational Mobility." *American Sociological Review* (February 1960).

———, "The Extended Family and Geographical Mobility." *American Sociological Review* (June 1960).

LOPATA, HELENA ZNANIECKI, *Occupation Housewife.* New York, Oxford University Press, 1971.

LYNN, D. B., A note on sex differences in the development of masculine and feminine identification. *Psychological Review,* Vol. 66 (1959).

"M," *The Sensuous Man.* London, Corgi Books, 1972.

MAGARSHACK, DAVID, "Foreword" to his translation of Tolstoy's *Anna Karenina.* New York, New American Library, Signet Classics, 1961.

MALINOWSKI, B., *The Sexual Life of Savages.* London, Routledge, 1932.

MALLESON, JOAN, *Any Wife or Any Husband: Sexual Problems in Married Life.* London, Penguin, 1966.

MERSH, IVAN N., "Personal and Social Influences in the Development of Gender Identity," in Ormsted and Taylor.

MICHELS, R., *Political Parties.* Collier Books, Edition N.Y. 1962, original 1915.

MILL, JOHN STUART, *The Subjection of Women.*

MILLETT, KATE, *Sexual Politics.* London, Hart-Davis, 1971 (New York, Doubleday, 1970).

MITCHELL, JULIET, *Woman's Estate.* London, Penguin, 1971.

MONEY, JOHN, "Sexual Dimorphism and Homosexual Gender Identity." *Psychological Bulletin,* Vol. 74 (1970); *see also* Ehrhardt, A.A.

———, "The Influence of Hormones on Sexual Behaviour." *Annual Review of Medicine,* Vol. 16 (1965).

MORGAN, ROBIN (ed.), *Sisterhood is Powerful: An Anthology of Writings from the Women's Liberation Movement.* New York, Random House, Vintage Books, 1970.

OAKLEY, ANN, *Sex, Gender and Society.* London, Temple-Smith, 1972.

ORMSTED, CHRISTOPHER., and TAYLOR, DAVID C. (eds.), *Gender Differences: Their Ontogeny and Significance.* London, Churchill Livingstone, 1972.

———, "The Y-chromosome Message: A Point of View," in Ormsted and Taylor.

ORMSTED, MARGARET, "Gender and Intrauterine Growth," in Ormsted and Taylor.

ORWELL, GEORGE, *Inside the Whale and Other Essays.* London, Penguin, 1962.

————, *1984.* London, Penguin, 1957.

PARKER, TONY, *The Twisting Lane: Some Sex Offenders.* London, Panther, 1970.

PEEL, J., *see* Harrison, G. A.

PERRIS, G. H., *Germany and the German Emperor.* Andrew Melrose, 1914.

PHOENIX, C. H., GOY, R. W., GERALL, A. A., and YOUNG, W. C., "Organising Action of Prenatally Administered Testosterone Propionate on the Tissues Mediating Mating Behaviour in the Female Guinea Pig." *Endocrinology*, 65 (1969).

PIRANDELLO, LUIGI, "The Cooper's Cockerels," in *Pirandello's Short Stories*, translated by Frederick May. London, Oxford University Press, 1965.

PLATO, *The Symposium.* London, Penguin, 1951.

POLARI, P. E., "Sex Chromosome Anomalies," in Ormsted and Taylor.

POTTS, D. M., "Which Is the Weaker Sex?" in Harrison and Peel.

PUXON, M., and DAWKINS, S., "Non Consummation of Marriage." *Medicine, Science and the Law*, Vol. 4 (1964).

RAINONE, NANETTE, SHELLEY, MARTHA, and HART, LOIS, "Lesbians Are Sisters," in Tanner, Leslie B.

RAPOPORT, RHONA, *see* Fogarty, M.

RAPOPORT, ROBERT, *see* Fogarty, M.

RIESMAN, D., GLAZER, N., and DENNY, R., *The Lonely Crowd: A Study of the Changing American Character.* New Haven, Yale University Press, 1961.

ROKEACH, MILTON, *The Open and Closed Mind.* New York, Basic Books, 1960.

SCHAPIRO, T., *see* Gingsberg, G. L.

SCHOFIELD, M., *The Sexual Behaviour of Young People.* London, Pelican, 1968.

SCHUR, E. M., *Crimes without Victims.* Englewood, N.J., Prentice-Hall, 1965.

SELBY, HUBERT, *Last Exit to Brooklyn.* London, Corgi Books, 1970; Calder & Boyars, 1967 (New York, Grove, 1964).

SHELLEY, MARTHA, "Notes on a Radical Lesbian," in Morgan, Robin.

SHERRIFF, R. C., *Journey's End.* London, Heinemann Educational, 1958.

SIMENON, GEORGES, *The Door.* London, Penguin, 1968.

SLAUGHTER, D., *see* Dennis, M.

SOAL, BARBARA, *see* Abbot, Sidney.

SOLANAS, VALERIE, *S.C.U.M. Manifesto.* Olympia Press, 1971.

SOLZHENITSYN, ALEXANDER, *The First Circle.* Fontana, 1970.

SPIRO, M., *Children of the Kibbutz.* Cambridge, Mass., Harvard University Press, 1958.

STENGEL, ERWIN, *Suicide and Attempted Suicide.* London, Penguin, 1964.

STORR, ANTHONY, *Human Aggression.* London, Penguin, 1970.

TANNER, LESLIE B. (ed.), *Voices from Women's Liberation.* New York, New American Library, Signet, 1970.

TAYLOR, DAVID C., and ORMSTED, CHRISTOPHER, "The Nature of Gender Differences Explored Through Ontogenetic Analysis of Sex Ratios in Disease," in Ormsted and Taylor.

TIGER, LIONEL, *Men in Groups.* London, Nelson, 1970.

WALTERS, P., *see* Fogarty, M.

WEBER, MAX, *The Protestant Ethic and the Spirit of Capitalism.* London, Allen & Unwin, 1930.

WELLS, H. G., *The History of Mr. Polly.* London, Collins, 1910.

WHITE, R. J., Editor's Introduction to James Fitzjames Stephen, *Liberty, Equality and Fraternity.* Cambridge University Press, 1967.

WILLIAMS, A., *see* Gingsberg, G. L.

WILMOTT, P., *see* Young, M.

WOLFENDEN REPORT, THE, Report of the Committee on Homosexual Offences and Prostitution, 1957, HMSO, Cmnd 247.

YOUNG, J., *The Drug Takers.* London, Paladin, 1971.

YOUNG, M., and WILMOTT, P., *Family and Kinship in East London.* London, Routledge and Kegan Paul, 1957.

———, *Family and Class in a London Suburb.* London, Routledge and Kegan Paul, 1960.

YOUNG, W. C., *see* Phoenix, C. H.

ZIMMERMAN, R. R., *see* Harlow, H. F.

About the Author

ARIANNA STASSINOPOULOS was born in Athens in July 1950. She was educated in Greece and won an Exhibition to Girton College, Cambridge. In 1971 she was President of the Cambridge Union. She graduated with honors in economics in 1972 and is now at the London School of Economics preparing her Ph.D. thesis on the Mediterranean Countries and the Common Market.